Ingrid,
Thank you
my Child

12/10/19

KL

Childish

Stories from the Life of
a Young Black Girl

KishaLynn Moore Elliott

This autobiographical book reflects the author's present recollection of personal experiences over time. Portions of these stories have been fictionalized. Events have been compressed and dialogue has been recreated. Names and identifying details have been changed to protect the privacy of individuals.

CreateSpace Independent Publishing Platform

www.ChildishTheBook.com

ISBN: 9781727614688

DEDICATION

This book is dedicated to my late grandmother Anne Ruth Stevens Moore Combs (1927-1997) and to her son, my late father, Scott Langston Moore (1957-2015).

ACKNOWLEDGEMENTS

Thank you to my mother, Monica Billups, without whom I would not be here to live, to write or to share any stories. My childhood was difficult for us both. Our healing continues. I love you and I honor you.

To my wife, Shelli Elliott, who gave me our beautiful son, Simeon, and all the support I needed to make this next D.R.E.A.M. come true. I love you more than yesterday, but not as much as I will love you tomorrow.

To my mentor and editor, Sanda Balaban, my most trusted advocate, and an indelible believer in my craft. Our story is still unwritten, but I'm willing to wait for it. I love you.

I'd also like to thank Shamera Reid (@iiampoetiic) for the cover illustration, and Ghia Larkins (@imagesbyghia) for the author photographs.

Table Of Contents

Prologue: Child Of A Child

I once saw my own creation in a dream. I was walking alongside God, who was a Light. I walked with this Light into a large room with rows of people in it, paired in twos. Together, God and I strolled through the room, examining each couple.

God and I both stopped before an attractive couple. The woman's face had the shine of youth to it. Her eyes were the color of chewy caramel candies. The man's skin bore the patina of scars from minor car crashes, but his mocha smile was bordered with charming dimples.

They appeared to be an unlikely match for each other in age and personality. Yet for some reason, God and I agreed that they were perfect for me. So God, as Light, reached out and touched the woman on her heart. I was transported from God's side into her womb, carrying a beam of God's Light with me.

It turned out that the shine of youth in my mother's face came from her being a child herself when she became pregnant with me at the tender age of 17. She had her own twisted tales of growing up too soon. She had dreams. She had talents she was just discovering, as we all do at that age. A kid would ruin everything. Motherhood wasn't in the plan for her.

My father, while a bonafide adult at age 25, was hardly mature enough to help raise a child. He had a good paying job, a motorcycle, and multiple girlfriends. He compelled my mother to empty her womb. Fatherhood wasn't in the plan for him.

But God's Light stayed with me, growing stronger and brighter within my mother until it reached her heart again, just in the nick of time.

She didn't have the abortion.

I was born on September 6, 1980 with my mother's dazzling eyes, with my father's flirtatious smile and with my own resilient spirit. This began my journey as Kisha Moore, the child of a child and a man who didn't want a child.

Let's see how this goes.

###

LIVING IS PAINFUL

Some people don't remember their early childhood. Others remember happy moments of Christmases, birthdays, or vacations with friends and family.

My memories of childhood begin in 1983 at age three, when my father kicked down the door of our house in Columbus, Ohio.

The tune of "Suicide Is Painless", the opening theme to *MASH,* a TV show about US soldiers in a medical unit that I inexplicably loved, had just begun to ring out from the small color TV in the living room where I was sitting. Suddenly, a foot crashed through the bottom panel of the front door. I jumped up and screamed for my mother, who appeared at the top of the stairs just as my father breached the entry with the rest of his tall and lean body. He began shouting at my mother, who rushed down the stairs screaming back at him.

I began to cry as they collided into a fistfight. I reached up to grab my father's arm while he loaded it up to throw a punch at my mother. He twisted his arm from my grasp with such power that my three-year-old body went flying back onto the couch. I curled into a ball and helplessly watched him pick my mother up and slam her body down onto the ground like a wrestler. I couldn't distinguish my cries and screams from hers. I pinched my eyes closed, covered my ears, and waited for the violence to end.

Later that night, I cuddled in the arms of my father's mother, Grandma Ruth. I felt safe with her. That safety eased my sadness as she helped me understand that my parents were getting a divorce.

"They love you very much." She said. "They just can't get along with each other. They never should have gotten married in the first place."

I referred to this as "The Divorce Fight" for the rest of my childhood. I never watched *MASH* again.

After my parents divorced, my mother and I moved into a house across the street from her older sister in the Franklin Park neighborhood of Columbus's near east side. My only friends at that time were my five cousins—three of them were children of my mother's older sister, and the other two were children of my father's sister.

Together we all tried our best to be children. We played make-believe and tried to create happy memories. But those memories faded against the backdrop of our parents' constant drama. Fighting and substance abuse surrounded us, robbing us of safe spaces both in our homes and just outside of them. Screams, sirens, and flashing red lights stole many nights of sleep from us.

My cousins and I shared the experience of poverty together, bonding over food, whether it was penny candy from the market on the corner, or slices of government cheese when it was delivered to our doorsteps each month. Good days were defined not by the joy we felt, or by the fun we experienced, but by whether or not we got to eat a hot meal. As an only child, I was grateful to have my cousins around. It was a cold world to face alone while my mother worked to provide for us.

I rarely saw my father. When he did make an appearance, it wasn't to spend any time with me. He would ride his motorcycle up to our house every so often. I could hear its roar crescendo in our direction from blocks away. He would park it outside, leave it running, hop off and run up the stairs. He would stay only long enough to throw a wad of cash and a hateful glare at my mother, before riding away again into the night.

Hi Daddy…bye Daddy.

My mother had moved on to a new boyfriend. He was a smooth-talking bartender named Harry. He always smelled like liquor and cigarettes. He taught me how to ride a bicycle without training wheels when I was five years old. I almost liked him.

Then Harry broke into our house one night while I was sleeping with my mother in her bed. A noise at the window at the foot of the bed woke me. I saw a strange shadow at the corner of the window. I shook my mother awake just as the window screeched open and the shadow climbed into the room. My mother jumped up, and the terrible shouting began.

It was completely dark in the room. I hid under the covers, afraid to see or be seen while I listened to my mother and Harry scream at each other. I was crying out for anyone to come and help us. Suddenly, our next-door neighbor burst through our front door and into the bedroom. Even in the dark, I could make out the shape of a gun, pointed directly at Harry.

"Get out," our armed angel said to Harry.

Harry leaped back out the bedroom window and took off running. My mother rushed over to the bed and told me to go across the street to my aunt's house.

"But I'm naked." I protested, still crying. She jerked the bed sheet off the mattress and tossed it at me.

"Go Kisha! Right now!" she screamed.

I tiptoed in a rush across the street, barefoot, nude, draped in the sheet and in tears. My mom's sister already had her door open. I slipped into her dark house and joined my cousins in their bedroom where they had slept peacefully through our living nightmare.

Not long after the Harry break-in, my mom decided that we would move from Ohio to Tampa, Florida. Her mother, my Grandma Beth, lived there and was battling breast cancer for the second time. She needed care. We needed to escape the bleakness of Columbus. So my mother packed us up, and I said goodbye to my cousins.

Then in the middle of an Ohio winter night in 1985, we departed on a grueling 15-hour ride on a Greyhound bus. My mom and I left Columbus and its old pains behind, gearing up to face new ones in the south.

###

Sex Ed

I have always loved girls. It started at age six, in my 2nd-grade classroom in Tampa, where I made my first best friend. She was a petite and pasty white girl named Julie. Julie had a glorious mane of red wavy hair. When the light caught her amber locks just right, it would sparkle.

We used to crawl under the table at school together and sing. Sometimes we would hold hands and giggle at the chocolate/vanilla swirl our laced fingers created. Under the table with Julie in 1986, I felt alive. With her, I was a happy and innocent child. I wanted to live there with her forever and avoid the things awaiting me outside of the safety we created for each other in that space. Sadly, we moved to a new apartment, and I changed schools, leaving Julie behind, but not the memories of our moments.

I knew well enough that boys went with girls and girls went with boys. No one around me spoke about gay people, or about being gay. I had no cause to question my fondness for girls because I hadn't been exposed to anything to awaken my sexual curiosity.

When I entered 3rd grade in 1987, Grandma Beth relocated to

an assisted living facility. My mother and I moved into a second-floor apartment in a large complex. My mom struck up a fast friendship with our next-door neighbor, Jean. Mom and Jean used to go out together a lot. When they had plans to hit the town, my mother would leave me in the care of the two sisters named Shanice and Shantay, who lived in the apartment just across from us. Shanice, the older sister, was tall and gangly. Her younger sister, Shantay, was shorter and thicker. Both of them were teenagers, with hickory skin and Jheri curls. Their loud voices annoyed me, so I usually kept to myself in my room while they watched me, shutting their loudness outside.

They usually didn't bother me when they babysat me. But one evening the sisters started coming into my room, wanting to play. They had awkward games, including one they called 'Telephone'. Shanice would go first, whispering something into my ear. Then I would have to whisper the same thing, no matter how raunchy, to Shantay. Shantay would then whisper something back for me to pass on to Shanice. The game would continue with me delivering the dirty messages between them until they got bored. The game didn't bother me, even though I could sense it was taboo. I felt curious. I didn't understand all of the things that I was repeating. I recognized some words, such as "breasts" and "kiss". I knew "fuck" and "ass" were curse words. I figured out what "pussy" was pretty quickly. The words were just words to me. The sisters never touched me, so I allowed the game to go on and kept it to myself.

After a few more babysitting shifts, they introduced a new game called, '7 Minutes In Heaven'. For that game, we would sit in the dark in my bedroom closet together. My closet was too small for both of them to sit in it with me so they would take turns switching in and out. Together we would sit in my closet, close enough to each other that I could hear breathing, but dark enough that I couldn't see what was happening.

There was no touching in the closet. Just more whispers of dirty words and heavy breathing. I didn't like the game, mostly because I was afraid of the dark. But since one of them was always in there with me, I was able to tolerate the time in awkward blackness until they were each done and it was over.

I never told my mom what was happening. I started to ask to stay by myself instead of with the sisters, but my mom refused, saying age seven was too young to be left alone. Soon the time came again for my mother and Jean to go out. Shanice and Shantay arrived to watch me, filling our apartment with their dark, loud bodies. That evening, they joined me in my room to play. We played a few rounds of 'Telephone' first, and then on to '7 Minutes in Heaven'. On this particular night, the game had a different ending.

I was in the closet with Shanice, listening to her whispers and heavy breathing.

"I don't want to play this game anymore," I whispered to her in the dark.

"What? I thought you liked it," she said. I heard panic in Shanice's voice.

“Not really. It’s boring. Can we stop?”

“Are you going to tell your mother?

“No. I won’t tell.” I promised. “But I want to get out now.”

We opened the door to exit the closet. Shantay was lying on my bed. Her pants were down, and I could see her full, naked privates on display before me. It was brown with folds of pink, covered on top in strands of shiny black hair. Shanice got very upset. I stood agape while she rushed over and grabbed her Shantay off the bed.

“Pull up your pants!” she said before dragging her sister out of my room. I stayed behind, confused by the scene.

Why did she have her pants down?

I never found out.

The sisters never babysat me again, even though I never said anything about it to my mother. I stayed curious about what made a girl breathe heavily in the dark.

My mother only had one sex talk with me, when I was eight years old. I sat between on her legs on the floor as she brushed my thick, curly hair into submission, and asked her how babies were made.

"Babies are made by having sex, which is only something adults do," she started. "Each month, a woman's body releases an egg into her womb."

I imagined a chicken egg, floating in every woman's stomach.

"If that egg is fertilized by sperm during sex, it makes a baby," she continued. "If not, it breaks down and bleeds out of the vagina. That's called a period. When you become a woman, you will start having a period," she finished.

For a long time, I thought that egg yolks leaked out of women on their periods. It sounded gross.

During those early years in Tampa, my only friend was my cousin Nicole. Nicole taught me everything else there was to know about sex. During our many sleepovers, we whispered in the night about the naughty things that happen with boys. My mother had never explained penises or intercourse to me. Nicole explained to me how penises and ejaculation worked in vivid detail. She also taught me about masturbation.

"Have you ever looked at your coochie?" asked Nicole while we were playing in her room on one lazy Sunday afternoon.

"What do you mean look at it?" I asked.

"I mean, looked at it in the mirror. Up close?"

"No. Why would look at my coochie in the mirror?"

"To know what it looks like," she said.

That made sense to me. I had seen Shantay's vagina. I might as well have a look at my own.

Soon Nicole and I we were taking turns standing over handheld mirrors, looking at our vaginas.

"Mine looks kind of lopsided," I said, staring at my smooth, but uneven labia closely. I handed the mirror over to her. She had a look.

"Mine looks normal," she said.

Of course it does. I didn't check to see for myself.

"Did you know it feels good to touch it?" she asked.

"I'm not touching my coochie!" I answered.

"Well, if you do, it's normal. It's called masturbation. And it feels good."

I decided to take her word for it at the moment. But as soon as I was alone again in the bathroom, I sat on the toilet with my legs apart and dipped my index finger deep into my vagina. It didn't feel good or bad to me. I pulled my finger out and examined it. It was moistened with creamy mucus. I gave it a sniff. It was odorless. Next, I did what felt logical to me. I stuck out my tongue and tapped it against my finger for a quick taste. It was very tart.

I got off the toilet and washed my hands. I wasn't sure if I had done masturbation right, but I knew I felt guilty about it. I heard the rumors about the fast girls at school, but I didn't aspire to be like them.

When I entered 4th grade, Grandma Beth's second battle with breast cancer took a turn for the worse. She moved back in with my mother and I and started receiving hospice care. She was prone to mean, verbal outbursts, which I forgave due to her deteriorating physical condition. On weekdays, I had to spend three hours alone with her each day until my mother got home from work. I tried to stay quiet and keep my distance to avoid interactions with her. It didn't always work.

One afternoon she called for me from her bedroom just as I walked in the door from school. She was usually asleep when I got home, but there was no such reprieve for me this time.

"Kisha! Come here you little whore!" she shouted.

Bright lights bothered Grandma Beth's eyes. When I walked into her room, it was dark except for the bit of light shining around the perimeter of her window curtains.

"Them little friends you got is nasty," she said.

"Friends?" I replied. It was genuine confusion. I had no friends in Tampa except for my cousin, Nicole. Yes, there were other children in my apartment complex, but they were hardly my friends. They were bullies who taunted me relentlessly during the long walk home from school.

"I just heard them talking about finger fucking in the hallway," Grandma Beth accused.

"What...what is finger fucking?" I asked.

"YOU KNOW WHAT IT IS!" She screamed back at me. I was startled for a second but recovered quickly. I was used to her yelling by then. She screamed at my mother all the time.

"I don't know what you're talking about Grandma. I just got home. I was alone. There's no one out there," I said.

"Well, I heard 'em. And you can't play with them nasty friends of yours no more."

I didn't argue with her. I could hardly protest losing something I didn't have in the first place.

"Yes Grandma," I said, before slowly backing out of her room.

Later that night on the phone, I asked my cousin Nicole what finger fucking was. She explained it in explicit detail. On hearing it all, I agreed with Grandma Beth—it was nasty! So much about sex seemed confusing.

These were things I didn't need to understand as a child anyway. Not yet. I would have plenty of time to learn about sex and sexuality. Besides, I knew that sex was misbehavior for everyone but adults. I did my best to stay out of all kinds of trouble. Some feared God. Some feared monsters.

I feared my mother more than both.

###

FOSTERED

My eyelids peeled open, expecting to take in the familiar darkness of my bedroom. Instead, they met with two pairs of strange eyes staring back at me. The resulting jolt of fear and confusion stunned me into a recollection of the events of the previous night—a Friday in the early spring of 1989.

In a flash, my mind rewound, and then slowly replayed the scene of Friday afternoon, with me walking quickly and anxiously down the road home from school.

My bullies were in tow, jeering from an ever-closing distance. The long way, straight down the road, was hopeless. They would catch up. The shorter route, through the woods, was dangerous. They would catch up. Before I could make up my mind what to do, they caught up.

The bullies did what bullies do. They bullied. I did what the bullied do. I cried and didn't fight back. Once my tears satisfied their collective hunger for creating misery in the lives of those weaker than them, they ran off. I continued home, slowly. I took the long way down the road. I saw no sense in adding to the danger I was already in for being late getting home from school.

It a long journey that I was permitted a strict 30 minutes to make.

Oh well. I'm already on punishment for not completing my homework and getting bad grades. How much worse can it get?

I was not at all prepared for the absolute rage in my mother's eyes when I finally stepped across the threshold of our apartment, an hour late.

"WHAT THE FUCK TOOK YOU SO LONG TO GET HOME FROM SCHOOL?" she screamed.

I highly doubted that explaining a bully delay would help my cause. My mom had no tolerance for my failing to fight back against any abuser that wasn't her. So I said nothing. Regardless, my plight immediately worsened. My mother dragged me into her bedroom and soon I was emitting chilling screams of anguish from a beating.

My mother's instrument of choice on that day was a six-foot-long pink leather belt that had holes along its entire length. It was designed to wrap multiple times around a curvy body over a cute dress. Instead, it was wrapping around the tender flesh of my 8-year-old thighs, back, arms, and anywhere else my mother could aim and attack.

The tap at the bedroom door was an initial relief. It was the hospice nurse who was administering in-home palliative care to Grandma Beth, who was losing her second battle with breast cancer. Even the nurse seemed to shrink from the rage in my mother's glare, but she stood her ground as she informed my mom that as a mandated reporter, she was obligated to notify the authorities of all instances of abuse. My mother's words were as cold and clear as ice.

"Do what you have to do," she said.

Then my mother slammed the door in the nurse's face, ending my reprieve. She continued the whipping for a few more lashes until she grew weary from the exertion.

The police arrived before my tears could dry. Suddenly I was suffocating in the cramped space of my grandmother's bedroom, being questioned by two cops.

"Do you feel safe here?" the cops asked. I took a look around at the intense stares from two cops, a concerned hospice worker, a dying grandmother, and an angry mother. My answer was clear.

"No," I said.

Who knew that one tiny word could do so much?

I learned quickly and had plenty of time to contemplate the lesson as I was escorted into the back of a police car like a criminal. My school bullies, who lived in the same apartment complex, watched, pointed, and laughed, unknowing and uncaring of the trouble they had caused.

I was dropped off at the Florida Department of Children and Families headquarters. There was a long wait in an empty room filled with toys that I did not play with. Just as I began to wonder if I would have to sleep in that playroom, a middle-aged black man with salt and pepper hair on his head walked in and introduced himself as Greg, my social worker. I followed Greg to a smaller office where he invited me to have a seat.

Greg had a beard, which he stroked while he sat at his desk and worked the phones, seeking placements for me. A while later, he escorted me to his car, and we took a long drive out to Lord-Knows-Where, Florida in the middle of the night. When we finally arrived at the home, a pleasantly round Black woman with short grey hair escorted me into the back door of it.

“I'm Mrs. Stevie James. You can call me Stevie," she said, with a warm smile. “Come on," she said, taking my 8-year-old hand. “I'll show you to your room.”

My memories ended and I was back to being stared at by strange children in a strange home. From the cot, I faced the four curious eyes staring down at me. They looked on silently as I sat up and assessed my situation. I addressed the older one first.

"Where am I?" I asked.

She said nothing.

"She can't hear or speak." the younger one said. "She's Deaf."

She pointed to her ear, then her mouth. I'd later learn this as the America Sign Language (ASL) sign for 'Deaf'.

"My name is Sabrina," said the younger girl. This is my sister Tamika."

"Hi," I said, slowly. "I'm Kisha."

I was still processing Tamika's deafness when Stevie entered the room.

"Ahh, Kisha. I see you're up. Long night for you. How did you sleep?" she asked.

I couldn't answer because at that moment I couldn't recall sleep at all. I remained silent. Fortunately Sabrina was there to speak for us all.

"She just woke up!" Sabrina exclaimed. "I introduced us, and told her she is Deaf," she gestured towards Tamika, who stood here still staring at me.

"Well, come on and meet the boys," said Stevie.

Boys? I stepped off the cot and followed Stevie out of the room with the two other girls in tow.

There were twelve of us in total—nine black boys and three black girls. One of the boys was Stevie's biological grandson. The rest of the children were the same thing I had become—foster children.

I thought I would be given a safe place to stay for a night or two—long enough for my mom to calm down, forgive me, and love me again. But as Saturday and Sunday passed, it was clear that I wouldn't be going home immediately, or even soon. That Monday, I stood at a bus stop outside the door of my new home, with several of my new siblings, and was carted off to a strange new school. The only thing I was sure of was that I had begun a bizarre new life—one in which I was no longer an only child.

The concept of having sisters and brothers was exciting to me. I quickly adapted to my situation over the days that followed. I got to know my foster siblings, all of whom had heartbreaking stories of physical abuse and traumatic loss.

I learned that Tamika and Sabrina were biological sisters, and one of the boys was their biological younger brother. It was Sabrina who informed me of this and many other facts. She talked almost non-stop. It seemed as though she'd been blessed with the words of which Tamika, her older, Deaf, mute sister had been robbed. Sabrina was determined to use every one of those words each day, twice.

Right from the start, I was desperate to communicate with Tamika. I felt like we had things in common despite our one glaring difference. At 11, she was closer to me in age than her 6-year-old sister. She was big for her age too. And neither of us knew how to speak up for ourselves.

I was pretty shocked to learn that no one in the household knew sign language except for Tamika, the Deaf girl. As such, no one could really communicate with her beyond crude points and gestures, and she couldn't talk with anyone beyond the same. She relied on passing notes. All Sabrina knew were the most basic signs and how to fingerspell the alphabet. After a week in foster care, I learned how to fingerspell as well.

Unlike the others, I began using finger spelling rather than miming and gesturing to communicate with Tamika. In turn, she would teach me how to sign the words I spelled. It wasn't long before Tamika and I were able to carry out a complete conversation in American Sign Language.

Once Stevie discovered that I had acquired this skill, she deemed me to be the household sign language interpreter. I was honored to step into the role. It gave me a purpose for the indefinite amount of time I would remain in foster care. It gave my foster sister Tamika ears and a voice. More importantly, it made me Stevie's automatic favorite! I had grown quite fond of my foster mom.

Stevie James was a devout Jehovah's Witness. We spent every Sunday in Kingdom Hall, where she sang the hymns loudly. Her favorite hymn was "Life With No End—At Last!". It was about finding peace, paradise, and everlasting life with Jehovah for all those who joined. I was a believer right away. I wasn't scared of death, but I definitely wanted peace and paradise. I also wanted to bond with my foster mother by spending as much time with her as possible. So I became a devout Jehovah's Witness as well. She would take me on special outings to bible studies and conventions. I felt very special.

Stevie was married to a farmer whose first name I never learned. Each day my foster father was up and out of the house before dawn. Stevie made sure us kids had all gone to bed long before he got home from the farm, even if it meant there was still daylight out at bedtime.

Stevie and her husband were wealthier than any black couple I'd ever known. Shortly after I was placed with her, we moved into a brand new house they were having built out in the country, closer to the farm.

One Saturday, Stevie loaded us all into her large van and we took a family ride out to see progress on the home. It was tough for me to imagine that the massive slabs of concrete and wooden beams the construction workers were nailing together would become a home. But two months later, we were all moving in.

The home had a brand new smell. To an eight-year-old, it looked like a mansion—opulent, beautiful, with large rooms, chandeliers, red carpeting, and a converted garage for us foster kids to play in. Outside it sat on acres of land with a forest of trees expanding on every side as far as my young eyes could see. Inside, it had much more space than Stevie's previous home. Whole portions of the house were off limits to us foster children, so I wasn't sure how many rooms there were in total. I still shared a bedroom with my two foster sisters. The nine boys could now be spread out, three to a room instead of six.

The house featured an enormous dining room with a table

that could fit 16 people—all 12 of us foster children, Stevie, her two live-in adult children, Chris and Katherine, and Mr. James, her husband, who would only join us when Stevie cooked his favorite meal, 'Crab Shala'. This succulent dish was made of spaghetti topped with crab legs cooked in a spicy sauce. It was my favorite meal as well. That dining room table was the only place I'd ever have it.

Once we were in the new house, weeks flew by. Every night I spent precious moments huddled in a corner in the garage with Tamika, learning to sign under her tutelage. We were both studying a thick three-ring binder full of American Sign Language vocabulary.
One day, Tamika asked me to help her speak.

"How do you say this word?" she signed, pointing to a picture of a house in the ASL vocabulary binder.

"House," I said the word aloud.

She immediately mimicked the motion of my lips, but no sound came out.

"Breathe out hard when you say it," I signed to her.

She tried again, and this time an audible "how" sounding wind blew from her lips.

"Very good!" I signed to her enthusiastically.

She smiled. That's when I started teaching Tamika to talk

during our nightly lessons. For every word she would teach me in ASL, I would work with her to speak it out loud. I realized I could improve her life by teaching her to talk.

Or so I thought.

A week later, I walked into my foster home from school to find Stevie and Tamika sitting with a white woman in the living room. They all looked very upset. Tamika would not look at me. The white woman glared at me. Stevie had a mixture of sadness and stress on her face.

"What's wrong?" I asked.

Before my foster mother could answer, the white woman stood up and approached me.

"Have you been teaching Tamika how to speak out loud?" she demanded, pointing an accusing finger at my older foster sister.

"Well yes," I answered, proudly. "She asked me to. She's been teaching me sign---"

The white woman cut me off and addressed my foster mother in clipped tones.

"You see?" she said. "I knew it. This is a disruption and clear violation of our school policy. If she's caught attempting to speak out loud at school again, she will be expelled." Then she marched to the door and let herself out without saying goodbye.

I was baffled. Later in life, I would learn to understand why it is vital in Deaf culture to use sign language, not speaking, to communicate. No one explained it to me at that moment though. I looked at my foster mother.

"Keep learning to sign," Stevie said. "No more speech lessons though." She let out a sigh.

I was horrified.

Later that night, huddled in our corner with our three-ring binder, Tamika wept silently.

"I will still teach you to speak." I signed to her with all the passion my hands could muster.

"No." She signed the word back to me with a crisp snatch of three fingers.

I understood that she was afraid. If she got in trouble at school, it could jeopardize her placement. She was willing to stay silent to avoid being separated from her brother and sister.

I signed back, "If you can't speak, then neither can I."

For the next week, I refused to communicate in anything but ASL or writing at home in the act of silent solidarity with Tamika. Stevie understood and supported it. My foster siblings even tried to join in, but none of them could keep their mouths shut. It became a fun game for us to play to see how long we could all remain quiet. Sabrina always lost; I always won.

I was in foster care for a few more weeks. My fourth grade school year ended, and we were all sent to summer day camp. One night my social worker Greg called to say he'd be picking me up for a court date the following day. He had already picked me up three times before that to take me back to the Florida Department of Children and Families building for awkward supervised visits with my mom. I had been in foster care for almost six months. Even though it seemed like my mother and I were better off without each other, Stevie started hinting that I might be going home soon.

The thought of leaving her home saddened me, but I knew the day would come eventually. It was too good to be true otherwise. I was fortunate to be placed with Stevie. Some of my siblings had been in the system for years. They told me horror stories about placements that were worse than their situations at home. We all knew that we were lucky. Most foster homes didn't have chandeliers in the dining room and forests in the backyard. My foster siblings also helped me to see how good I had it. My situation with my mother was temporary; most of them were never going home again. The more I learned, the more I felt like I was taking up space of a child who might really need it.

The next day, my foster siblings went to day camp while I sat outside a courtroom by myself on a bench. My social worker had already gone inside with my mother, but children weren't allowed inside the courtroom, so I had been asked to wait outside. I was trying not to die of boredom when a white lady with blonde hair approached me.

“Excuse me. Are you Kisha?” she asked.

She looked familiar. I realized I had seen my mother talking to her sometimes when my social worker and I arrived for our visitations.

"Yes," I answered.

“Wow, you look just like your mother.” She said. I was used to hearing that. I just sat there, looking down.

“Well, good luck today! I think your mom is going to get to take you home. Oh, and I’m very sorry for your loss,” she said.

Now I looked up at her.

“What loss?” I asked.

“Your grandmother, Beth. She passed away recently?”

The words died off in her throat, which she cleared quickly. “You didn’t know?” she stammered.

I could barely hear her, as my young brain tried to process this information. Grandma Beth was dead. I never got to say goodbye or grieve. The last word my grandmother heard me say was the "No" that had me whisked away by the cops. I began to cry, and the white woman backed slowly away before rushing off.

The doors of the courtroom opened, and my mother and my

social worker stepped through them. Both of them were smiling, but there I wept on the courthouse bench.

“Why didn’t anyone tell me Grandma Beth died?” I cried.

"Oh, honey…" my mom responding, giving me a hug of comfort. "I’m sorry. I wanted to tell you myself, I just couldn’t contact you or see you until today. Yes, Grandma Beth passed away a few weeks ago. She was very sick. She just couldn’t fight anymore.”

I was trying to compose myself when Greg, my social worker, interjected with what he thought was good news.

“The judge approved your release from foster care,” he announced cheerfully. “You will be returning home to your mother today. We’re going to go get your things right now. I should have had you pack them before we left.”

It was too much loss for a child to handle at once. Grandma Beth was gone and now I had to say goodbye to Stevie and my foster siblings as well. My mom was still holding me. I sobbed into her shoulder.

When I was calm again, Greg and I said a temporary goodbye to my mother. Then, he drove me back to my foster home one last time to pack up my things and say goodbye. Unfortunately when we arrived, my siblings were all still at day camp. I would never see any of them again. I was fine with that. It was hard enough facing Stevie for the last time.

Stevie gave me a large pillowcase to gather the few things I had accumulated over the six months I was there. She also gave me a long hug goodbye. It didn't seem easy for her to let me go, but she did not cry. I could tell she was used to this process; it came with the territory.

That evening, life resumed back under my mother's roof. The only thing I found joy in was seeing our dog, Windsor. My mother had bought an adorable Shih Tzu puppy on her birthday the week before I was placed in foster care. He had been so tiny I could fit him in the palm of my hand. His tongue dangled out of the left side of his mouth—a permanent defect. I thought it was cute. It was instant love for me with this puppy. Seeing him again was a shock. He had grown to almost full-size. I was delighted to see Windsor. I'd virtually forgotten about him during my time away.

I was heartbroken to see my late Grandma Beth's vacant room. I was surprised that her death was affecting me so much. It was the first significant death I had experienced. I didn't have a single positive memory of her from our time in Tampa. It had been hard watching her battle her illness and my mother at the same time. She had been mean to me, always treated me suspiciously and accused me of heinous misbehaviors. Yet I believed somewhere in there she loved me, even though I couldn't remember her ever saying so. I would miss her.

I was also not happy about meeting Tommy. Tommy was a new boyfriend my mother started dating while I was in foster care. He let himself into our apartment that night.

“Where my pussy at?” he called out.

He stopped short when he saw me sitting in the center of an air mattress on the floor in the living room. I hadn’t been ready to sleep in my dead grandmother’s bedroom, so my mom had set me up out there.

He stared at me like I was a total surprise—not just my presence, but also my existence. The feeling was mutual on my end. My mom hadn’t mentioned that she was expecting a guest. I instantly disliked him. My mom rushed out of the bedroom.

"We need to talk," she said, grabbing his hand, pulling him with her into the bedroom. She closed the door behind them, and it remained closed for the rest of the night, leaving me alone on the floor in the living room on my first night back from foster care.

Some welcome home. I thought. I don’t know why I hoped things would be different. I deeply missed Stevie James and the company of my foster siblings.

Windsor stood up and shook himself out, and then gave himself a long stretch and a yawn before climbing up on the air mattress to lie beside me. At least I had my dog to bring me some joy. I would certainly need him.

A couple months later, my mother and I moved in with Tommy, and I started fifth grade at a new school. I was not happy about Tommy being a permanent fixture in our lives.

At school, I became fast friends with an Asian girl named May. We bonded over our unhappiness at home. Neither of us got along with our moms. We both hated our mother's boyfriends in particular. So, I hatched a plan to run away and return to the safety and comfort of Stevie James's home. I quickly recruited May as my accomplice for the mission.

We set a specific date and time when we would leave our homes forever, raising 9-year-old middle fingers to our moms, their boyfriends, and our misery. The plan was to pack enough clothes, essentials, and food to survive for two weeks. We would meet each other at a school bus stop, celebrate freedom, and then figure out the rest from there. May had been saving her allowance and had accumulated close to $200. That was a fortune to us. I believed it was enough money for us to make it to Stevie James's house, once we somehow managed to find it. I was certain she could foster us both in her massive home.

Each day leading up to our rebellious rendezvous, I spent some time packing. One benefit of moving in with Tommy is that we could afford a spiffier apartment. My bedroom even had its own bathroom. It also had a large walk-in closet where I staged my runaway provisions. I had a huge suitcase, which was strange, since I never traveled anywhere. The luggage was bright red leather, and when opened it was equal to the size of two regular suitcases. I decided to use one half of it to store my clothes.

Should I bring shorts and skirts or just jeans? I wondered. I finally chose to pack appropriately for all weather. Who knew where we would end up or what the climate would be like there?

In the other half of the suitcase, I was trying, in vain, to fit all of my other valuable essentials. These amounted to books and music, which I couldn't live without. They were my only sources of joy at home, besides Windsor, whom I couldn't take with me. I rotated items from my book and cassette collection in and out of the suitcase, my priorities shifting like the tides. Then I remembered I needed to save space for food. Since May had money and I didn't, I had agreed to bring the food.

I believed that food was going to be the least challenging part of the plan. I waited until the Sunday night of our escape to pack. We never had very much food in the house, but it was my luck that my mother had just gone grocery shopping. The fridge and cabinets were filled with ample sustenance for me to share with May.

I stayed up past my bedtime, quivering inside with excitement at my impending escape. From my room, I listened for my mother to go to bed. I grew nervous watching the minutes tick by on the clock through the 10 o'clock hour. May and I had agreed to meet at midnight and take it from there. It was almost 11:00 PM when my mom finally retired to bed. I waited for what I felt was a reasonable amount of time before tiptoeing from my bedroom into the kitchen.

My strategy was simple. I would take everything we could eat without cooking. I opened the cabinets and made my selections of cereal, bread, canned veggies, and beans, laying them out on the counter. Next came the refrigerator, from which I pulled all the lunchmeat and cheese, condiments, milk, and a 2-liter bottle of soda.

May and I will eat so well! I thought.

I was contemplating whether or not to take cooked leftovers of mom's spaghetti when suddenly the dining room light switched on and I heard my mother's voice.

"What in the hell are you doing?" she asked.

I froze. Busted. Terrified. My mind had to work quickly. It's not like I could say "packing food so I can run away with my friend May." So I lied and told her the next best thing.

"I was hungry," I answered.

My mother's eyes, framed by arched eyebrows and fatigue, panned over the two counters full of food.

"Why did you pull out all this food?" she said to me. I could hear disbelief in her voice.

"I was going to eat it," I said, following the lie.

"ALL of it?" She sounded distraught.

I felt so ashamed that I forgot about running away for a moment. I lowered my eyes.

“Yeah,” I mumbled.

I braced myself for her fury. I wondered if she was going to beat me again. But instead of yelling, or rushing me, she was silent. I studied her face, and on it was a look of sheer concern.

"Go to bed." She said, clearly disappointed.

I could hardly believe it, but I didn't need to be told twice. I slipped past my mom and rushed back to the safety of my bedroom, with my packed luggage waiting inside it on my bed. I had to abort the mission. I had no way to reach May and let her know. I could only hope she had made it out—or didn't.

The mystery was solved the next morning at school. We both exchanged relieved looks as we slid into our respective assigned classroom seats.

“You couldn't go through with it?” She whispered.

"No, I got caught. What happened to you?" I whispered back.

“My mom stayed up all night. It's like she knew or something,” May said with a sigh.

I shared the story of being busted preparing a smorgasbord of food for us. We laughed about our unfortunate circumstances.

"You are lucky," May said. "My mother would have killed

me!"

"I was scared!" I told her. "I thought for sure that I was going to catch a beat down. But she didn't even yell at me."

"Well," said May, "she was probably scared you'd get taken away again."

That had never occurred to me. I felt like my mother regretted that I was back at home as much as I did, especially with Tommy in the picture.

It didn't matter. I had to accept that there would be no returning to Stevie James's home. My mother, her boyfriend, and everything else were pieces of the life I had been dealt. My best bet was to foster my own endurance to tolerate it all.

###

Fighting For AJ

In 1991 my mom and I moved to a new apartment. We had lived in Tampa for five years but had we moved around town eight times since, constantly changing residences and schools. I never knew when or why a move was coming. I learned not to ask questions or complain. It wouldn't help.

The apartment complex that we had just moved from was very nice, with playgrounds, a pool, and a beautiful lake that I loved to sit beside on a warm day.

This new apartment complex was more like a cheap two-story motel. One upper apartment was stacked on top of a lower apartment, both packed between apartments on either side, all wrapped around the complex's only amenity—a central parking lot. That was my new playground.

Things were contentious between my mother's boyfriend Tommy and I. He had popped up the night I was returned to my mother from foster care, and never left. While most of my mother's romantic relationships were short-lived, theirs had persisted for almost two years by then. Tommy and I couldn't stand being in the same room together. He complained that he couldn't talk about grown folks business when I was around. I didn't know what my mother saw in him. We regularly dueled for her attention. I was frustrated because he always seemed to win the battle. I spent evenings and weekends alone in my room while Tommy dominated our TV, our home, and my mother's love.

I was more isolated than ever and desperate to make more friends. I had attended three different schools in the fifth grade. My mother moved us around, chasing Tommy and evading follow-up visits from the Florida Department of Children and Families. The days I was in school were rough. I was that awkward black girl, always reading a book or humming music or daydreaming. These were not the hobbies of cool kids in the fifth grade. I was also getting fat, as result of my new habit of overeating. I tried to ignore the extra weight and the names the mean girls called me at school. There were many school days when the sounds of kids laughing at me drove me to tears. I was relieved when the summer began—summers meant a break from being teased at school, and more sleepovers with my cousin, Nicole, my closest friend. She and I spent as much time together as our moms would allow.

One summer day I was gazing out of our apartment window when I noticed new neighbors were moving into the apartment above us. I eyeballed the family. They were a black couple with a pair of kids—a young girl and a teenage boy. I almost died of joy as I watched them move in. I made my way outside to say hello.

The young girl, Crystal was entering the 6th grade in the fall, just like me. When I first laid eyes on Crystal, a plump and pretty black girl with peanut butter skin and beautifully braided hair, I knew I wanted her to be my best friend.

Her older brother's name was Anthony, but he went by AJ. My heart gasped when I met AJ. He was drop-dead gorgeous. His stature was short, but carried himself tall, with a cocky smile, a faded haircut, oversized clothes and the smoothest cacao skin I'd ever seen. Hormone surges tortured my pre-teen lady parts at the mere sight of him. It was instant love. I had to have them both, if at all possible.

Good fortune was on my side. The woman in the couple was their mother; the man was their mom's boyfriend. My mother met their mom, and they became fast friends, as did their respective boyfriends. Soon we were hanging out in each other's apartments all the time. Inevitably Crystal, AJ, and I would be told to go away and play.

My crush on AJ made it hard to speak to him, but Crystal and I struck up a conversation quickly. She laughed when I confessed that I was head over heels in love with her bother. She was used to girls having crushes on her brother, so it didn't bother her. Crystal and I would watch TV together, or watch AJ play video games while we made girl talk. It was a beautiful friendship.

Nicole lived far across town. It was nice to have Crystal as my best friend, living right upstairs, because we could see each other all the time. She was going to be attending my school in the fall.

AJ would be entering 8th grade and starting junior high school, just like my cousin Nicole. The remaining weeks of summer gave me a great head start with building a friendship with Crystal. By the time school started, we had already claimed each other as best friends. That also increased my confidence. Most of the bullying stopped.

Most of it.

However, there was one gnarly and loud girl named Ebony who persisted in her bullying. She got on and off the school bus at the stop just before Crystal's and mine. Every day as I boarded the bus, Ebony's meanness would begin as either a silent glare or threatening gesture, or a verbal insult or jab that made everyone in earshot laugh at me. Crystal encouraged me to ignore her, which I did. But her threatening behavior got under my skin. I had no idea why she hated me so much, or what made her choose me as her target for constant harassment so early in the school year.

Crystal and I always sat together on the school bus, heads together in giggling conversation. One day on the bus, Crystal gave me a Polaroid photograph of her brother. In the photo, AJ was crouched down low and pouting like he was LL Cool J. The drool had barely begun to pool in my mouth when Ebony ripped the picture from my hands from the seat in front of us.

"Who is this?" she demanded.

"That's my brother AJ." Crystal answered.

"Man, he's FINE!!" she said, waving the photo around so her groupie friends could see.

"That's mine!" I finally spoke up. She looked down at me and seemed surprised that I had found words and dared to speak them.

"Well it's mine now, ugly!" she said. "So is he. If I even so much as hear you speak his name, I'll beat your ass!"

Something in me snapped. I didn't just want my photo back. I wanted AJ. She hadn't even met him!

I'll be damned if I let this ashy, skinny nobody try and take him away from me. I thought. I decided to take a stand.

I rose from my seat, and with all the defiance I could muster, I screamed.

"AJ!!!!!!!!!!! AJ! AJ! AJ! AYYYYYEEEEE JAAAAAYYYY!!!"

A stunned silence fell over the bus. From that moment, I knew it was on. Ebony knew it. Crystal knew it. Everyone left on the bus knew it, except for the oblivious driver, who slowed the large vehicle to a creaky pause at Ebony's stop. As she and her friends got off the bus, she left me with a chilling threat.

"Tomorrow, your ass is mine!"

Crystal and I were silent as we got off at the last stop and started a somber stroll back to our apartments.

"I'm sorry she took your picture," she said softly.

"It's ok," I said sadly. I was much more concerned about the impending fight. I had never been in a fight before, outside of a few shoving matches with Nicole, which I always lost. There was no chance of my mom helping to protect me. She had been disappointed in me when I told her I was being bullied in school at the end of 5th grade.

"You need to take a sock to school and put a large rock in it," she would advise. "The next time they start messing with you, bash the biggest one in the face with it. Then the rest of them will leave you alone."

I couldn't imagine doing such a thing. Instead, I stopped telling her about my bully troubles at school.

Still, I was sure that Ebony would destroy me in the next day's scheduled bout. I needed a form of rescue from the situation. So, I went to my mother, taking advantage of the chance to talk to her before Tommy got home from work.

"Mom, I have a problem." I started.

"What's going on?" she asked.

"Well, there's this girl from school. She rides the bus with Crystal and I. She's super mean, and now she's threatening to beat me up tomorrow. I don't want to fight her. Can I skip school tomorrow? Please?"

My mother sighed.

“How many times do I have to tell you that running away doesn’t solve anything? You have to stand up for yourself. The only way people will stop messing with you is if you show them that you can’t be messed with,” she said.

“But, mom…” I pleaded.

“No buts. I’ll tell you what. Not only are you going to school tomorrow," my mom said, her eyebrows arching sky high, “but I am going to be waiting at your bus stop when you get home. And if you don't stand up to that girl, you'll have to stand up to me.”

I regretted saying anything. Now I was trapped between the threats of two bullies. I cried myself to sleep that night.

The next morning I woke up and got ready for school, still trying to plot my way out of this fight. I dressed up in clothes that weren’t appropriate for fighting—a skirt, a button-down blouse with a vest over it and patent leather shoes. I looked like I was going to church instead of to my own execution.

By the time Crystal and I got on the bus, word about the fight had spread to the rest of the kids. I could tell by the looks on some of their faces that they were surprised I showed up to school. What they didn’t know was that I was much more afraid my mother than of Ebony, who stared daggers at me as Crystal and I made our way to our seat on the bus.

The bus groaned up to the school and let us out. I prayed to

God that Ebony wouldn't start this fight with me on campus. I didn't want to get suspended. When we got off the bus though, she walked on, ignoring me. I went through my school day under assumed safety. I even began to wonder if I was off the hook. I knew I wasn't when at lunch she flipped me the finger, then sliced it across her throat while mouthing the word "Later."

On the bus ride home from school, there was loud chatter about the upcoming bout. As Ebony and her goons got off at the bus stop before mine, I heard her directing them to follow the bus down the road. They all started walking.

I was terrified. I felt there was no way I could win this fight. My only remaining option was to try and run to my apartment from the bus stop before they caught up to us.

All hopes of doing that died when the bus pulled up to our stop. My mother was home from work early, sitting there as she had promised, wearing a tank top, cut-off shorts, and a scowl. I couldn't believe my misfortune as my eyes went from her to Ebony, who was approaching.

"What the hell are you wearing? Those aren't fighting clothes!" my mother scolded me.

Before I could answer, Ebony and her entourage had arrived. I sized her up. We were evenly matched in size—in fact, I was bigger than her. But she had a large crowd with her, while I only had Crystal in my corner, along with my mom who was also, presumably, on my side. My mother looked me in my eyes to deliver her final words of advice.

“Wait until she touches you, and then you kick her ass." She said, before giving me a shove towards my opponent.

I stared at Ebony, who glared back. Standing there in the surreal off, I realized that I wasn't sure how a fight should begin or end. I was just waiting for something to happen when suddenly Ebony started stepping towards me.

"I heard you talking shit! What's up now?" she yelled, throwing up her arms.

"I wasn't talking shit!” I yelled back, glancing over at my mother apologetically for cursing, "You were!"

She stepped closer to me.

"What up now you fat bitch?" she yelled. The small group of kids offered a collective "Oooo”! That hyped her up, and she took a step closer. I stood my ground silently.

“I told you I was gonna beat that ass! You thought I was playing?” she hollered.

Now she was so close that I could smell her breath. In the next moment, she bumped her belly into mine.

She touched you! Kick her ass! I thought.

My brain quickly turned the signal into action. I took a swing and hit her soundly in the center of her chest, pushing her back a few steps. I could tell she was surprised. I was too. The stunned moment didn't last long.

She launched herself at me, and soon we were locked into a scuffle, surrounded by a crowd of boisterous children and my mother. I pulled Ebony's hair. She kicked me in the shin. We punched at each other, but nothing seemed to land. I managed to grab hold of her hand and bend her fingers back. She yelped and leaned over, firmly biting my arm through my blouse sleeve. We broke apart in pain, both gasping for breath. Then, I steadied myself and put up my dukes. She advanced again, still flying off at the mouth.

"If you pop my fucking chain, I swear to God!" she yelled.

As she got within arm's reach, I noticed the delicate gold chain and letter "E" charm glittering around her neck. She had exposed herself. I seized the opportunity. As she reared her arm back to take a swing at me, my arm reached out to block. In the same motion, I quickly grasped the chain, pulling it as hard as I could. It snapped off, and with a brief glimmer, its charm went flying.

"My chain!!" She screamed.

I took cover as she lobbed a few strikes down on me. I grabbed her arm and pull her down to the ground, returning counter swings, not even knowing or caring if they landed. The whole time my mom cheered rabidly from the sidelines.

"That's right! Show her!" my mom yelled as I continued to struggle with Ebony.

Both Ebony and I were getting winded and losing steam. I was beginning to wonder how this was supposed to end. Suddenly the crowded parted as a white man came running from across the street into the fight circle to break us up. Now my mother stepped in.

"Let them fight," she screamed at the man.

"Are you crazy? Why don't you stop these kids from fighting?" he yelled back at her.

"Why don't you mind your fucking business?" she hollered back.

The crowd's attention shifted to my mother and the man. For a moment it seemed like they would start a second fight. It was a welcome distraction. At that moment, Ebony and I reached a silent agreement that we were done fighting each other.

The crowd started to disperse. The white man saw that he had accomplished his good deed of stopping two black kids from fighting that day. He decided my mom was not worth the trouble and stormed off across the street.

I stood there with my mother, Crystal, and my bully, who was searching around on the ground for her jewelry. I wasn't sure what to do or say as I watched her.

“Sorry about your chain," I said. Then I turned and walked away. My mom and Crystal followed.

“I'm proud of you for standing up for yourself, Kisha.” my mother said as we walked along.

I stayed quiet. I didn't feel very proud. I was just relieved that it was over.

Later that night AJ showed up at our front door. I was shocked to see him when I answered.

"Crystal told me what happened." He said. "That's pretty cool that you care enough to get in a fight over a picture of me. She told me the girl took it, so here."

He handed me another Polaroid photo of himself. This time he was standing, with a goofy smile that made me melt. I thanked him, and he said goodnight, turning to leave. I couldn't believe my luck.

The following Monday, Crystal and I walked up to the bus stop. I was surprised when some of the kids there smiled and said hello to me. That was very unusual. That's when one of them told us that I had been declared to be the winner of the fight because I threw the first punch and I popped her chain. I didn’t know the rules of school fights, but I was incredulous that I could win one. As the school bus pulled up, I was dreading what would happen when I laid eyes on Ebony. But instead of a glare, she actually smiled at me. I smiled back.

My mother was right about one thing. I didn't have any more problems with school bullying during the 6th grade. Ebony never bothered me again. Word got around about the fight and about my crazy mother. Even though no one messed with me, I wasn't any more popular at school. Crystal remained my only friend on campus. I didn't care. She and AJ were all I needed. I also had my cousin Nicole.

Then I made the unfortunate mistake of introducing Nicole to AJ during a weekend sleepover at my house. I had invited Crystal and AJ downstairs to hang out on a Friday night. There was instant chemistry between the Nicole and AJ the moment I introduced them. They could feel it; I could see it. Nicole's eyes went glossy, and AJ's face bore his goofiest grin while they shook hands. Of course, I wasn't surprised that AJ liked Nicole. She was his age, and far more beautiful than me. Besides, every boy wanted Nicole.

What I wasn't expecting was for Nicole to betray me with mutual feelings for AJ. She knew the depth of my feelings for him. She knew that I had recently won a fight over him. None of that stopped her from making out with him at my sleepover. Crystal and I left them alone in the living room for a few minutes and returned to find them kissing on the couch. I was furious, but I waited until Crystal and AJ left to confront Nicole about it.

"How could you do this? You know how I feel about him!" I screamed in her face the moment after Crystal and AJ had gone home.

"You guys aren't dating! What's the big deal?" she replied.

"The big deal is he's mine! I knew him first."

"He is not yours. Knowing him first doesn't make him yours. Dating him makes him yours. Are you saying you're dating him?"

"You know I'm not dating him! But that doesn't mean you can. You can have any boy you want. Why do you have to take AJ from me?"

"I can't take someone you don't have, cuz."

I snapped and rushed at Nicole. I had never won a physical fight with her before, but I had also never been this angry before either. I landed on her with the full force of my body. Totally caught off guard, she went crashing to the floor. I pounced on top of her, slapping at her hysterically until my mother, raised from her slumber by all the noise, pulled me off of her.

"What the hell is going on with you two?" my mother demanded.

"I HATE HER!" I screamed.

"Kisha, calm down! I mean it!" my mother warned.

Nicole was still on the floor, holding her ankle and wincing in pain. My mom went over to check on her, inspecting her ankle.

"It hurts!" Nicole cried as I rolled my eyes, still fuming from across the room.

My mom touched her way around the ankle while Nicole whined painful protests.

"I think it's sprained. God damn it, Kisha, we're going to have to take her to the doctor!"

"I hope it's broken," I said, before storming off to my room, shutting and locking the door behind me. I no longer cared what happened to Nicole. My faith in our friendship was shattered. She could sleep on the floor, or in the trashcan, for all I cared. She was garbage.

The next day Nicole went home from our weekend sleepover a day early, with an elastic bandage wrapped around her ankle. My mom put me on punishment for two weeks.

"Save the fighting for bullies. Not your family," she said.

I wasn't allowed to make phone calls, go out or have visitors, which mean I couldn't see Crystal or AJ outside of school. I barely cared. Crystal and I still had our bus ride. I had nowhere else to go and no one else to see now that Nicole was dead to me.

I tried not to think about AJ too much. He was never going to be mine, so there was no point in fighting for him anymore.

###

O, Hi, Oh

Like many children of divorced parents, I would often fantasize about living with my non-custodial parent—my father. In the summer of 1992, my wish came true. My mother put me on a plane to go live with my father for the next two years. The plan was for me to stay with him and my stepmother, Yvonne, through 7th and 8th grade, and then return to live with her in high school.

Shortly after I left Tampa for Columbus, my mother married Tommy, and they moved to his hometown—San Antonio, Texas. I wasn't thrilled with the news, but I was too far from my mother and too safe from Tommy's insolence to care. Tommy, Texas, and my mom all were as irrelevant to me as I was to them. I had Ohio; I was home.

I was ecstatic to be back in Columbus with my Grandma Ruth, my cousins, my aunts, and most importantly, my father. I had made a few short summer visits to Columbus in the years since my mom and I had moved. However, this time I was allowed to stay and experience all the seasons. I was overjoyed to feel the nights grow cold and to watch the days get short. I was determined to make the most of this opportunity to remain for a while. I wanted to enjoy life and experience the pleasures of childhood for once.

I didn't get to enjoy it for long. By the time school started, I was twelve years old and puberty had found me. I started my period, which was accompanied by painful cramps and acne on a monthly basis. I cringed when I asked my father for money to buy pads. Yvonne didn't get periods, so she didn't buy them. My father gave me $20 and we never spoke about it again.

While my peers around me were getting growth spurts. I was just getting fat. I had always been tall and big for my age, but puberty brought with it more emotional eating and weight gain. I was the fattest student in my 7th-grade class. As my weight grew, my self-esteem plummeted. Bullies can smell low self-esteem from a mile away. I had moved halfway across the country, but the target on my back had come along for the journey. It took its share of hits.

My biggest bully that year was Cynthia, a popular mean girl on campus who lived in the same apartment complex as I. She was very light-skinned and slim. Her hair was always freshly styled in fashionable looks—high ponytails, finger waves, and gelled edges coiled into intricate designs around her hairline. I thought she was beautiful until the bullying began.

At school she was a terror, teasing, pushing, and provoking me on the playground and during the walk home. Her favorite thing to do was pull my dress up to expose my underwear to our classmates.

"Rag check!" she'd yell, speculating about whether or not I was on my period. If I was, there was no hiding the bulge of a maxi pad in my crotch. Their laughter would ring in my ears. I started being ashamed to have my period.

Years of bullying had taught me a few evasion tricks. I stopped wearing dresses to school. I avoided the playground at lunch and recess. I strategically trailed behind Cynthia on the walk home to prevent harassment. Eventually, she stopped bullying me. I was relieved when no one else filled the role that year.

I yearned for quality time with my father, but it was nonexistent. He worked the graveyard shift from 3-11 PM every weekday. He usually tacked on another 2-3 hours of overtime. Then, he'd hit the open road on his motorcycle for an hour or two. He would come home just before dawn. After having something to eat, he'd collapse into bed, sleeping until it was time to go to work again. On the weekends he slept throughout the day. My father was a night owl; he came alive after dark—after my bedtime. He would retreat to play his electric guitar in the basement until the sun came up. This had been his routine on his best days for years—he wasn't going to change it for his 12-year-old daughter.

I also shared my father's fleeting waking moments with insulin shock or "spazzing" as he called it. My father had been diagnosed with Type 1 diabetes at age 17. His condition was serious, but he never controlled it well. He despised sticking his fingers to check his blood sugar; it affected his guitar playing. He had a terrible habit of estimating his insulin dosages based on logic that no one else understood. Overeating food or having a higher than normal blood sugar made him feel sick. To avoid that, he would often overshoot the insulin, which would quickly burn through the glucose in his system. His body, without sugar, would shut down.

During his less serious spazz attacks, he would be incoherent and dazed until someone got some sugar in him through juice or popsicles. Sometimes, when his blood sugar was too low, he would fall out on the ground, thrashing violently to resist assistance with bringing him around.

During the worst spazzes, he would enter a coma-like state when his blood sugar dropped while sleeping. These were the scariest incidents for me as a child. There were many times when I was unable to wake my father and I had to call 911. Paramedics would arrive to administer glucose intravenously and save his life. We had countless "paramedics parties" as he called them, with plenty of spazz sessions in between. My father spazzed at least once a week.

Work, a motorcycle, sleep, diabetes, and a Gibson SG guitar were a lot to compete with for me. I was very disappointed at the lack of time with my father. I had been a daddy's girl when I was younger and craved any form of positive attention he gave me.

He preferred to provide me with his money instead of his time. My allowances stacked up quickly.

I didn't get much face time with my father, but my stepmother, Yvonne was always in my face. We had a strange relationship from the start. I liked her on most days, but she had weird mood swings. During her lows, she made me feel unwelcome and in the way. During her highs, she embraced me as her daughter, and asked me to call her "Mom." It felt unnatural for me, but I did what it took to stay on her good side.

Yvonne loved the TV show, *Law and Order.* We began to bond over the show, cuddling up in the bed she shared with my father to watch the show together. Each week I would bring a sugary bounty of candy, purchased with my generous allowance from my father. We would bet and barter lollipops based on whom we thought had committed the crimes in that week's episode. Towards the end of each episode, we'd bet double or nothing on whether we thought the jury would find the perpetrator guilty or innocent.

Those were pleasant memories for a while. Then everything changed. First, Yvonne's brother and niece started coming over frequently. Her family was from a tiny town on the outskirts of Columbus. I was relieved that we didn't see them often. When we did make the drive out to see them, it was always a miserable day of entertaining my stepmother's niece, JoJo.

JoJo was slightly older than I was, but a few grades behind

developmentally. She was a homely girl with a belly so round you would mistake her for pregnant if she wasn't such an obvious child. She commanded a lot more attention than I cared to give her. I tried to be nice to her, even though she depressed me. I was always relieved when my stepmother finally said it was time to go back home to the city.

Whenever Yvonne's brother showed up at our apartment, he and my stepmother would retreat into the basement together. My father had a man cave set up down there next to the washer and dryer. I sometimes spotted him in it while I did my laundry. He spent his waking hours on weekend evenings down there with his electric guitar plugged into his amp. Wearing massive headphones to seal in the music and block out the world, my father would play guitar and smoke marijuana for hours. I knew Yvonne and her brother weren't playing guitar in the basement, but the funky smell of smoke slipping beneath the bottom of the door gave me a clue about their chosen recreation.

They always left JoJo behind, grinning at me like a brown clown. I felt like a babysitter, even though I was younger in age. She spoke in simple sentences, sounding more like a 5-year-old than a 12-year-old. I could tell she looked up to me. She always found something about me to fixate on during our time together.

"I like your hair. Can you make mine look like that?" JoJo asked on one visit.

I had a relaxer in my hair, and wore it in a bob style, curling the ends with rollers every night. JoJo's hairstyle had gone out of style two years before. She had a greasy Jheri curl that barely reached her ears on either side. There was no chance of making her hair look like mine.

"No, JoJo. I can't. But we can watch TV." I told her.

The TV was always a good distraction for JoJo. We both liked to watch Beavis and Butthead on MTV. I would sit down on the couch. She would sit way too close beside me. If I let her, she might have crawled into my lap like a small child. I sighed and endured her violating my personal space while eyeing the basement door for her father and my stepmother to return.

Typically these visits happened once a month. But as the end of the school year approached, Yvonne's brother started coming more frequently. Sometimes they showed up twice a week.

After the visits, my stepmother was hyperactive and unpredictable. She would rush around erratically cleaning the house and snapping at me for being lazy.

"Why didn't you run the vacuum downstairs?" She demanded one day.

"I did run it," I answered, having finished all my chores hours earlier.

"Liar! Run the vacuum!" She shouted.

"I ran it already!" I cried back in confused frustration.

"Well run it again goddamn it! This floor is filthy!" She screamed, then storming off. I fumed in tears as I needlessly ran the vacuum downstairs again.

In a matter of weeks, Yvonne's physical appearance began to change. She had always been a slim, petite woman, but she became a sickly thin. The skin of her face looked like it was painted directly onto her skull as she lost the roundness from her cheeks. It scared me to look at her. Her anorexic appearance made sense. She had stopped cooking food and rarely ate. I had most of my meals at Grandma Ruth's, bought my own food, or fended for myself with groceries we kept on hand for my father.

The only foods Yvonne ate regularly were sweets. She was suddenly obsessed with candy. So much so that on our *Law and Order* nights, she started eating through all of the candy I brought without bothering to engage in our game of 'Who Did It?' Soon, I stopped showing up with candy on Thursday nights. She didn't seem to notice.

I tried to say something to my father, but he wouldn't hear me. He just told me to bear with her.

"She's a mess Dad. I never know which version of her I am coming home to!"

"She's had a rough time." He said. "It's hard for her to be around a kid. She always wanted one. She gave birth to a stillborn baby years ago."

"Oh," I said. "A dead baby?"

"Yeah," he continued. "Carried it the whole nine months." My dad's voice had softened.

"It wasn't my baby," he added. "It was before I even met her. But I think it always affected her. Some things you never get over. So, give her a break, ok baby? She really convinced me to bring you out here."

I agreed and tried to ignore his subtle admission that my presence in Columbus was never his idea or desire. I was here because Yvonne had agreed to take care of me. He was right. I decided to try and give Yvonne a break. After all, I liked her. She was a world better than Tommy. I could forgive some mood swings.

However, I couldn't overlook money disappearing from the Mason jar on my dresser. My weekly allowance was a generous $25. My father usually left a $20 bill and a $5 on my bed every week like a Payday Fairy. I had nothing to spend the money on but food, so I would put the $5 in my wallet as my snack fund, and stash the $20 in the jar as savings. The $20s built up quick. Every now and then I would count them. I knew I had well over $200 saved.

One day I noticed something bizarre as I glanced at the jar. Not only were there $20 bills missing, but there were also $5 and $1 bills. I always carried those in my wallet. I never stored them in the jar. It was as if someone had helped themselves to my money, but brought back change. I emptied the jar and counted the money. Almost $100 was missing.

I confronted Yvonne immediately.

“Hey, there is some money missing from my room. Did you take it?” I asked.

"No, I didn’t take your little money.” She said, rolling her eyes. I knew she was lying.

“Are you sure? Because I know there weren’t small bills in there. I only save the twenties. Now there are singles and fives in my jar.”

She said nothing, but I saw a flash of guilt cross her face.

“If you need to borrow some money, just ask—,“ I started before she exploded.

“I DON’T HAVE TO ASK YOU FOR SHIT! I FEED AND CLOTHE YOUR FAT ASS! I LET YOUR LAZY ASS STAY HERE! I DON’T OWE YOU A MOTHERFUCKING THING! GET OUT! GET OUT GET OUT!!” Yvonne screamed.

I quickly shrank away from her rage and rushed out. I hoped she only meant for me to leave her room and not all of Columbus.

From my room, I called Grandma Ruth, crying. I told her

what happened. I let it all spill out, about the mood swings, the candy, the visits from her brother and JoJo, and finally the money. Grandma Ruth listened patiently on the other end of the phone.

"Don't worry baby. I'll talk to your dad for you."

"Thank you Grandma." I sniffled.

My father could ignore me, but no man ignores his mother.

The next day I came home from school and was surprised to find my father sitting in the living room. He worked the night shift, clocking into work at 3pm, so he shouldn't have been there.

"Dad, are you ok?" I asked.

"No baby." He said. "Not at all."

I looked around and wondered for a moment if his blood sugar was low.

"Dad, are you spazzing?"

"No baby. I'm fine. Listen, I need you to go to stay at your grandma's tonight. Yvonne and I need to talk."

At that point, I figured Grandma Ruth had delivered my message. But I could sense that there was something bad happening. I had to wait until I got to my grandmother's house to find out what.

"She's a crack head," Grandma Ruth declared, taking a long drag from her Kool cigarette. My grandmother always cut to the chase and talked to me like I was a grown up. I loved her for it.

"You think she's smoking crack?" I asked. I couldn't imagine Yvonne smoking crack. She barely even drank alcohol.

"They are all on it. Yvonne, her brothers, our cousins. It's getting crazy, these new drugs. You used to have to worry about heroin and coke, but we couldn't afford that shit anyway. This stuff, it's cheap, the high is better than weed, but it doesn't last, so they just keep smoking and smoking it up. That's how they get you addicted." She took another long drag from her cigarette, which needed to be ashed. She often forgot this task, as evidenced by the many small holes tattooing her bed blankets and the couch upholstery.

"Grandma, ash your cigarette," I warned. She tapped its white tip into the ashtray on the table, picking up the glass of brandy next to it to carry with the cigarette back up to her mouth. She took a sip and a final drag before setting the glass back down and mashing out her smoke.

"What's gonna happen, Grandma?" I asked quietly.

"Well baby…" she began. I knew it wasn't going to be good. I braced myself.

"Once you get on crack, it's hard to get off. Your Dad and Yvonne might split up. If they do, he'll have to move back here and…" her voice trailed off while I filled in the blanks.

Grandma Ruth had tinnitus, is a terrible ringing in the ears. Her ringing was so severe that she constantly clicked her tongue to hear another controlled noise in place of it. It frayed her nerves to the point where she couldn't tolerate being around people for long—especially children. As much as she loved me, I couldn't live with her or even stay with her for more than a few days at a time.

"I'm going to have to leave, aren't I?" I said.

"Well don't worry about that yet, baby. Let's just see what happens. The school year is almost over. Nothing's going to change before that ends." She reassured me with soothing clicks of her tongue.

Everything changed though, immediately. When I returned home the following day, my father was there, again. It was the weekend, but he was usually asleep during the day. Sitting there on the couch, he looked like he hadn't slept in a month. I took a quick look around for Yvonne. There was no sign of her.

My father took a labored breath.

"It was Yvonne who stole your money." He announced. Then, he added. "She's a fucking crack head. She got fired from her job a few months ago and ever since she's just been smoking her way through our money, and now yours!"

I was shocked to hear about her job. She left to go

somewhere every day. I assumed it was to work. I was wrong.

"Today, when I searched the house I found a crack pipe in the basement. Then I went and I found her at a crack house, down the street from mom's," he continued.

"Is that what she and her brother do down there when he comes over? Smoke…crack?" I said, putting the pieces of this sordid puzzle together in my head. It wasn't marijuana after all.

"Yeah." He confirmed. His head dropped down to his chest. There was more.

"I'm moving. We can't afford to stay here anymore. I kicked Yvonne out. So...you're going to have to go to back to live with your mom."

There was a quiver of sorrow in his voice, and I wondered if he had been crying. I had witnessed my father physically disabled by his diabetes many times in my life. This was the first time I was seeing him in real emotional distress. For a daddy's girl like me, it was a dreadful feeling that punched me in the gut. Though this was terrible news, I could feel sorry for myself later. I knew he needed me to be strong.

I walked over to the couch and climbed onto it next to him, leaning over to hug my head against his chest. He wrapped his arm around me, and we breathed through the struggle together. I knew I was losing Columbus, but my father was losing his wife, his home, and his child all at once.

School ended two weeks later. I was surprised when my father showed up to my 7th-grade promotion ceremony and proudly watched me receive an Honor Roll award. The next day, we started packing up the apartment together. My father boxed up his and Yvonne's things and I packed myself in suitcases and boxes to be shipped to Texas.

I was granted a last-minute reprieve from a summer of Texas heat when my mother's oldest sister Brenda agreed to take me in for the summer, extending my time in Ohio. She was my favorite aunt. Her only child, my cousin, Nathan, was my best friend in Columbus. The invitation to stay with them felt like a miracle, and I was grateful for it.

That summer, I got saved and baptized at church.

Temporary salvation from Texas wasn't the only thing that drew me to the baptism pool. Aunt Brenda was an apostolic minister and evangelist. My cousin Nathan played drums in the church band. They both took church very seriously, and so did I. Spending every Sunday that summer at the Church of God in Christ, the Word of God made its way into my heart.

One of the reasons I got swept away in Christianity was that it inspired me to believe that I was a rapture away from the end of all my misery. Christians of the Apostolic faith believe in baptism by water and by the Holy Spirit, or speaking in tongues. We were taught that the rapture would randomly happen in the blink of an eye. Jesus would return like a thief in the night to gather His saved. The unsaved would rot, forever left behind in Hell.

I believed I needed the blood of Jesus to carry me through all that lay ahead in Texas, which sounded like Hell on earth to me. I decided I was ready to accept Jesus Christ as Lord. I told Aunt Brenda that I wanted to get saved. She and my cousin Nathan were elated.

On the day of my salvation and baptism, I confessed all my sins to Jesus in prayer and repented. These sins primarily consisted of impure thoughts about sex, girl crushes, and occasional masturbation. At the altar, I asked to be born again, be made new, and be redeemed by the blood of Christ. Deacons prayed for me as I sealed the deal verbally, accepting Jesus as my personal Lord and Savior.

Then Aunt Brenda led me out of the sanctuary and up some stairs to a small room. She and fellow evangelists help change me into baptism clothes. I was going to be baptized immediately. I was lost in a spiritual reverie of prayer and redemption, so I allowed myself to be puppet-mastered through the motions of my baptism preparation. Soon it was time for me to mount the stairs into the baptism pool. I could see the church pastor standing there at the top of the steps, ready to douse me in the holy waters in front of the entire congregation. Behind him, a massive cross was mounted to the brick facade of the wall. My legs shook as I climbed the four steps up, reaching for my pastor's hands.

The church music, led by the confident percussive rhythms of my cousin Nathan on drums, swelled to a sanctified gospel peak. From over the glass that bordered the pool, I could see the sweaty black faces of the church congregants. Their arms were raised, giving glory to the Lord for their salvation as I received mine. They were shouting, falling out, and praising the Lord. I was praising Him too.

Hallelujah Lord. Forgive me of my sins Lord. Baptize me in Your holy water. Fill me with Your Holy Ghost and save me.

The pastor dunked me down in the water in Jesus' name. I honestly felt reborn when he lifted me back up. The congregation went wild with praise. It all faded to the background as Aunt Brenda hurried up the stairs to receive me from the pastor. She and the other evangelists huddled around my dripping wet body, mumbling in prayer.

I was led to sit on a chair. I was crying with joy and gratitude for my new relationship with God. Little did I know, my love for the Lord was about to be tested.

"Now that you have received Baptism by water, it's time for you to receive the Holy Ghost, as evidenced by the speaking in tongues, as the Lord gives the utterance," Aunt Brenda said. "Open your mouth and invite the Holy Spirit into your heart."

The evangelists all joined hands around me. I realized their mumbling was actually praying in the spirit. Now I was expected to do the same.

I was nervous about this step, but surrender was the point of the whole process. So I allowed myself to let go, surrendering myself to the spiritual energy of the moment. Then I opened my mouth and spoke in tongues for several minutes, surprising even myself.

Aunt Brenda was very proud of me. Later that night she presented me with a pink leather bible, which she inscribed on the inside with the date of my salvation, baptism and receiving of the Holy Ghost—August 1, 1993.

A few days later, with teary eyes, I hugged my father goodbye at the airport while Aunt Brenda and Grandma Ruth watched. I felt bitter to be leaving him a full year earlier than planned.

As I boarded my flight, clutching my pink bible to my chest, I also felt hopeful that I wasn't facing whatever awaited me in Texas alone. I had a lot more faith in Jesus than I had in my mother, in Tommy, or in myself.

###

RUNAWAY

It started out as a good day. Those were far and few between for me in 1994 during eighth grade in Texas. I had asked my mother to do my hair, and she had agreed. That was a big win with my stepfather around. He hated when she would pay any kind of attention to me. And yet, I had prevailed on this day. I felt gleeful as my mom applied chemicals that would burn my kinky hair into straight submission. When the relaxer had done its magic, she blow-dried my hair into silky stiff lines, which I greased and wrapped on pink foam rollers that clipped into place around my curls.

Suddenly my stepfather got in my face, demanding that I unload the washer and dryer. I took issue with that because he was doing the wash, not me. Why did I have to finish it for him?

It wouldn't have been so bad if I hadn't hated my stepfather from the moment I met him the day I came home from my foster home four years before. My hatred only deepened when he had the gall to marry my mother and move us to his hometown of San Antonio, Texas. I hated Texas almost as much as I hated him. You could tell the feeling was mutual by the way he moped and whined whenever I was in the room or whenever my mother would spend a second with or a dollar on me. It was a constant battle of wits—one I always believed I was already winning because he was battling a child. What man of any intelligence does that?

But on this night he took it too far.

“Kisha, go make yourself useful!” he demanded. “And don't think you're cute because you got your nappy little hair done."

His insult pushed me over the edge.

"Fuck you!" I screamed, drawing my mother’s attention from the living room. She sprang to Tommy’s defense, as usual.

"Have you lost your mind? Who are you talking to like that?" she asked.

"Him! I hate him, and I am not doing his laundry!" I shouted.

"Yes you are if you know what's good for you!" she retorted.

"I don't care what you do to me, I am not washing his clothes. If you have to spank me then so be it!"

My mom pounced at me, grabbing my arm and dragging me back to my bedroom.

"You think you too grown and big for me to beat your ass, but I will show you!" she warned.

My stepfather smirked at me as he took off his belt. I glared back, wishing I could use it to choke him. Instead, I braced myself for the hits. My mom reared back with the belt and hit me with it twice before I jumped up in pain. That's when my stepfather reached out and grabbed me, holding me so that my mom could continue the beating. This was the first time he had laid hands on me. I knew that there was no way I would let both of them abuse me. My brain switched from fight to flight.

Fortunately for me, he was a short and scrawny man. It didn't take much strength to escape his grasp. I shoved past him and made a run for the front door. I heard Tommy and my mother scrambling behind me as I raced towards it. Tommy reached the door just as I got it unlocked. I was able to open the door enough to wedge my leg through it. Then, Tommy he pushed hard on the door, slamming it into my knee, causing me blinding pain.

"LET ME GO!" I screamed. I could hear it ring out across the apartment corridor and echo down the stairs.

"Let her go," my mother said. Tommy released the door, and I fled.

I raced breathlessly down the stairs, my hair rollers bouncing up and down with each step I took. I reached the ground floor and was looking around hopelessly when a door opened. Our downstairs neighbors, a young black man and his girlfriend, stepped outside and quickly guided me into their apartment.

“We called the police,” his girlfriend said.

They comforted me while I wailed in emotional and physical pain. The police arrived at their place quickly. The tall white officer seemed to fill the whole space of the entry to their apartment when he came in the door.

This wasn't like the time I was placed in foster care at age eight. This officer wasn't as nice as the cops who had come to my rescue back then. He looked down at me, unsmiling, as I explained what happened. I was still sobbing as I spoke; my neighbor's girlfriend soothingly stroked my shoulder. The officer asked me to sit tight while he went upstairs to take statements from my mother and stepfather. It seemed like an eternity before he returned.

Are they going to take me back to foster care? I wondered. We were a long way from Tampa and my former foster mother.

By the time the officer came back, my tears had dried. He re-entered the apartment carrying a small bag.

"I'm gonna need you to come with me," he said.

"Where are we going? What did they say?" I asked.

"They said it is not a good idea for you to come home right now. I am going to take you somewhere you can be safe. Your mom packed you a bag of essentials," he said, lifting it. "Say thank you to these kind folks."

I thanked them and exited the apartment with the police officer. For the second time in my life, I was tucked into the back of a police car and driven away from my mother's house for my own safety.

I was surprised when I heard the officer radio in that he was taking me to a home for teen runaways. Runaways? I was sure I had heard him wrong. As much as I would have liked to run far away, I had barely reached the stairs. How could I be a runaway? I wasn't some insolent teen. My mother and stepfather were beating me; I left the apartment to escape abuse.

"Excuse me, sir." I chimed up from the back seat. "I'm not a runaway."

"Well young lady, it's clear that you left the apartment on your own, without permission. That, by definition, is running away." He explained. "You're a minor, and so for your safety, this place is your only option for the night."

I couldn't imagine what my mother told him. I tried to explain that I was being beaten. Apparently, he did not care; the information did not change our destination.

As I walked into the teen runaway home with him, I felt foolish for wishing to be taken away again. This place was no comparison to my foster home in Florida. It felt more like jail. The heavy steel doors at the entrance only had small windows at the center of each of them. It was dark inside on that night. Everyone else was in bed. There was a tiny office with a light glowing in the back corner of the building. That's where the police officer led me. A sleepy looking lady signed some papers the officer handed her and gave him a silent nod.

"You will be safe here," the officer said, handing me the bag my mother had packed.

"She will contact your mother tomorrow." He added before departing, leaving me with the lady in the office.

The lady sized me up quickly. I was quite a sight, standing there in a floral housedress that I wore as pajamas, slippers, and a head full of curls on foam rollers.

"Come on, I will show you to your bed," she said.

I followed slowly and fearfully behind her. She turned down a hallway and paused at the first door on the left before opening it.

"There. You're up top," she said, pointing into the room at a bunk bed that was barely illuminated by the dim hallway light.

"But, I'm scared of the top bunk," I said softly, gripping my bag tightly in my fists. It crinkled slightly.

"That's the only open bed we got. The bathroom is over there. You got five minutes to wash up, and then it's in bed till dawn. Lights out was an hour ago. Be quiet and don't wake anyone up," she said before she turned and left.

I followed the weak light into the bathroom. Walking in, I caught a glimpse of myself in the mirror. I saw rolled hair and bloodshot eyes producing fresh tears to join the ones that had dried on my face earlier. All I had at that moment was the pajamas on my back, and whatever was in the bag.

I opened the bag, which was way too light to contain anything essential. My light tears became gasping sobs as I saw that my mother had filled the bag with trash, and a hair comb. I knew she had done this on purpose. She had won. Now instead of being at home in my bed, or in a comfortable foster home with a loving foster family, I was in a city juvenile hall for runaways. My mother and Tommy had put me there.

I sat on the toilet in that bathroom and cried. Then I did something I hadn't done since I was baptized two years before. I prayed to God, speaking in tongues, begging for freedom and liberation. I remember wanting to implore Him in any language possible to save me; I hoped I was doing it right.

On that night, salvation meant staying where I was. I walked back down the hallway into my shared room. I climbed the bed ladder to the top bunk on wobbly legs, still praying to the Lord for deliverance.

There was no curious and gentle awakening the next morning, as there had been in my foster home. Sleepy darkness was flooded by a cruel glare as the lady who had received me the previous night switched all the lights on at once.

“Fifteen minutes to breakfast, let's go!” she shouted. I shot straight up in my bed, traumatized by the memory of the events leading to that point, and re-traumatized by my position on the top bunk. I stared down at the floor and found myself making eye contact with a dark brown Latina with long hair.

"What are you looking at heifer?" she asked.

My eyes quickly moved away and bounced around the room to the two other girls who were awakening there. One was white and the other was another Latina. I could tell that I was the youngest of all of them.

"You musta been the late arrival last night." one of them said. "What's your name?"

"Kisha," I answered.

"Yeah well, welcome to paradise Kisha."

The other girls laughed and then filed out to hit the bathroom. I remained frozen in my bed, scared to climb the ladder down from the top bunk, and scared to face what else lay beyond the door of that cramped room. I was in a home for runaway teens. That meant everyone else there was a runaway.

I found the courage to climb down out of bed. I walked towards the bathroom, which had been empty and eerie when I approached it the night before. It was now busy with activity, but I was no less afraid. There were six other girls in the home. As I approached, I heard them talking and laughing in the bathroom as if they all knew each other. No one acknowledged me when I entered the bathroom. Apparently, no one cared about a new arrival. I walked towards a sink, and then realized I had no toothbrush, no washcloth, no anything.

"Excuse me," I asked a girl brushing her hair nearby. "Do you know where I can get a toothbrush?"

"Try the store," she said. Another girl who was standing next to her burst out laughing.

"What's with the rollers?" asked a girl behind me. I ignored her and backtracked out of the bathroom. I went looking for the lady in the office. The door was closed, but I knocked on it anyway. I knew she had to be nearby since she had done the wake-up call.

When she opened the door, she looked supremely pissed.

"I'm sorry," I stammered. "I don't have anything with me. I don't even have clothes to put on."

"Didn't you pack a bag?" she asked.

"No. I didn't have time to. My mom packed me one, but…" My eyes filled with tears again.

She sighed and opened the office door wider. "Come in. You can look through the donations closet for some clothes and some hygiene products."

She opened a small door to a room that was full of shelves crammed with random items. There were open packages of socks next to open boxes of soap, and bags of clothes not sorted by type or size. I focused on clothes first. I was a big girl, weighing about 170 lbs. I was concerned about not finding clothes that fit.

My options were limited. I picked out a black t-shirt that had a gold design I liked and a black and gold skirt with an elastic waistband that I thought would fit. In one of the bags, I found a pair of flat brown shoes that didn't match the outfit but did fit my size 10 feet. I took a couple of socks and a bar of soap. Then I dug out a hand towel, a toothbrush, and a small tube of toothpaste. I looked for deodorant but didn’t find any. I said a prayer that that was all I would need to get through the day, and closed the closet door.

"Thank you," I said to the lady in the office quietly. She barely acknowledged me as I exited and returned to the now emptied bathroom. Time was up, and everyone else was gone.

“Five minutes!” the lady called after me.

I brushed my teeth and splashed water on my face, wiping it dry with the hand towel. Then I put on the clothes and slipped on the shoes.

Next, I ripped the rollers out of my hair. The act made me cry again. My hair had turned out beautifully. My locks looked far too cute for the terrible spot I was in. I gently combed the curls into place with the comb my mother had packed. Then I took a deep breath and sighed. If I had to be here, at least my hair looked pretty.

I was behind schedule, as the rest of the runaways had already finished breakfast as I entered the small cafeteria. The girls had been joined by a group of eight boys. I did the math. There were fifteen of us in total. I was the youngest at 13-years-old; their ages ranged from 15 to 17.

I wasn't hungry at all, so I grabbed an apple. I took two bites, which were a struggle to swallow down. I tossed the rest of it. Everyone was getting up, so I followed. They all seemed to know the routine already. I felt following along was the wise thing to do. A small group of students stayed behind in the kitchen washing dishes while the rest of us filed through a door at the rear of the kitchen.

The door led to a classroom. It was Monday—a school day. Much to my surprise, it looked just like a classroom I would have been sitting in if I had attended my school that day. There were more desks than students in the room. The desks were all lined up in rows facing a green chalkboard. A cluttered teacher's desk and some chairs were placed in front of that board.

A gruff looking white man with ginger hair and a five o'clock shadow on his cheeks, jaws, and neck sat in the chair. Everyone else took a seat, and so did I. The man waited a few moments silently. The rest of the group talked in low tones like they knew it wasn't allowed. No one spoke to me or seemed to notice my presence. I realized the teacher was waiting, as he would check his watch periodically.

It was evident to me we weren't all in the same grade. I was in 8th grade. These teens were already in high school. Some of them looked like seniors. I wondered how we could all be in the same class together? Soon the kitchen crew joined us in the classroom and took their seats. The teacher checked his watch one more time, cleared his throat, shuffled some papers and then began to take attendance. He called out names and each student responded "Here" when they heard theirs. My name was not called, so I raised my hand.

"I'll get to you," he barked. My hand fell from the air as if it had been shot.

"The rest of you, continue your assignments from Friday. When you have completed work, bring it to me, and I will give you your next assignment."

"Now, you." He pointed at me, then gestured me over with his index finger.

I approached his desk, feeling like everyone's eyes were on me. But, as I glanced around, most people were flipping through the notebooks they had retrieved from their desks. I took a seat in one of the small chairs next to his desk.

“What grade are you in?” the teacher asked me.

“8th grade,” I answered.

He opened a drawer in his desk, rifled through some files and then pulled out a folder. He flipped it open and thumbed through worksheets, counting out a few. He pulled these out and then replaced the folder in the file drawer.

"Here," he said as he reached over and handed me the worksheets and a notebook. "Do these. When you are done, bring them back to me, I'll grade them and give you more."

I walked the worksheets back to my desk and looked through them. One was an English assignment. One was a math assignment. One was a social studies assignment. All of them looked far below my grade level but I decided to take the easy out. I worked on the assignments, grateful to have anywhere else to focus my mind.

Within an hour, I was done with all three worksheets. When I turned them into him, he glanced at them quickly, checked them off, and handed me more from the file drawer. I wanted to ask if I passed them, but I could tell he barely cared. I decided not to care as well. I took the next batch of worksheets back to my desk. This time I worked more slowly on them. There was no reward for speed, ambition, or intelligence in this classroom. There was only compliance and credit. Everyone else seemed to go with it and worked quietly as well.

This went on for three hours. Then the teacher rose from his desk and dismissed us, asking students to bring any completed work to him. I joined a few students who walked completed worksheets up to his desk. Everyone else put their notebooks back in their desk and exited the room back into the kitchen, where lunch was served.

I was relieved that no one was speaking to me. I was accustomed to being bullied when I was younger so I preferred to be invisible. My invisibility paused for a moment when the lady from the office entered the cafeteria. We were eating what looked like microwave pizza and what tasted like crispy trash.

"Everybody," she said, gesturing my way, "this is Kisha. She arrived last night. She'll be on Group 2 for chores." After that grand introduction, she turned and left.

A few teens now stared at me without speaking. Their interest only lasted a moment before everyone went back to minding their own business. I went back to my fruitless effort to soften the pizza dough. I let it soak in my mouth for a minute before attempting to chew. It barely worked. I threw the rest of it away. I knew lunch was over when the group got up and started clearing out. The same group of students stayed behind to wash the lunch dishes. The rest exited the cafeteria into the main room.

The main room was a large room, set up like a recreation center. There was a pool table in the center of the room. In one corner, some chairs surrounded a small TV near the boys' hallway. There was a pair of double doors at the back center of the room. The lady's office was to the right of those doors. Shortly past that, the girls' hallway led past the two bedroom doors and ended at the bathroom.

I stood, surveying the place for a moment in front of the

cafeteria doors, which were centered between the girl's hallway, and the steel door through which I had entered the night before. Immediately adjacent to the exit door was a small conference room, surrounded by glass windows. It was sparsely furnished with a couch, some chairs, and a table.

A white girl approached me with a spray bottle filled with blue liquid and a rag.

"It's chores right now. You're Group 2. Today we clean the walls and windows." she said.

I looked around to see what the other groups were doing. One group was folding laundry on the pool table. My group's job was to wipe down all the doors, walls, and windows until they sparkled. I made myself busy with the task; I enjoyed it. Like the class worksheets, it was something easy to focus on. The dishwashing group soon finished its kitchen chores and headed out the double doors. With a small group of us working together, Group 2 breezed through the entire main room quickly. We too were free to exit through the double doors at the back.

The doors led outside, to an expansive, grassy fenced-in area, bordered with tall hedges that obscured our view of the outside world. There was a swing set at the back of the grounds and some tables and chairs scattered around the area.

Some of the teens hung out in groups of two or three. Most of the others wandered off by themselves. I walked alone toward the swing and sat on it. It creaked ominously under my weight. I felt the whole structure wobble as I took a tentative swing, pushing my foot off the soft ground beneath me. The chains groaned, protesting the motion. I figured the swing was more for looks than for use. I decided to sit there for a bit. I wondered what would happen next. After a while, the lady from the office emerged and called my name.

"Kisha, it's time to call home," she said.

I left the swing behind and went to her office.

The lady in the office reached for my file. She read it briefly, grabbed the phone, punched in some numbers, and then pressed the phone to her shoulder with her ear. She waited for an answer and asked for my mother as she continued thumbing through the report in my file.

"Yes, ma'am I am calling from Transitions. We're an emergency shelter for runaway youth. Your daughter Kisha was brought in last night and is here now. I was calling to see when we could set up a face-to-face to discuss what happened and how we can resolve it. When would you be free to come down?" Her face scrunched as she listened to my mother's reply. I couldn't make out what she was saying, but the lady's expression told me it wasn't good.

"Mmm hmmm. I see. Well, the city allows that youth can stay here a maximum of 30 days before they get referred to other services," the lady said.

My eyes widened in my skull.

"Either way we need to get you down here for a face-to-face. We can discuss what happens next then. Uh huh. Ok. I'll see you then."

She gave my mother the address, then looked over my file down at me.

"Do you want to talk to your mother?" she asked. I shook my head no.

"Ok goodbye, Ma'am." She said, and then hung up the phone. "Your mom said she would be here shortly. She is refusing to take you home at this point. You can return to recreation time. I'll let you know when she is here."

Darkness followed my heart back outside. My mom was going to leave me there. I would have bet my snake of a stepfather was dancing a two-step at this turn of events. He'd finally gotten rid of me. I could imagine him encouraging my mom to make me stay there. The rage that filled my heart then was so toxic that I felt sick in my stomach. What could I do? Nothing. I could do nothing but return to the swing and wait.

I was still in the swing when the doors opened a while later. The lady from the office announced it was dinnertime. We all made our way through the double doors.

"Kisha. Your mom is here. I am going to meet with her now. I'll call you when we're done." She told me as I walked by.

I walked through the main room, glancing only briefly at the office in time to catch a glimpse of my mother. She didn't look at me. I couldn't tell if she had seen me at all. I was so nervous that I couldn't eat dinner. I wasn't sure what would be worse at that instant—for my mom to leave me in the home, or for her to take me back home to my stepfather. I was mulling over this conflict when the lady from the office popped her head through the cafeteria doors and called for me.

"Your mom is waiting for you outside," she said.

I assumed that meant that I was leaving so I turned towards the exit doors when I left the cafeteria.

"No, she's out back," she said, then pointed to the double doors.

My heart sank into the floor. I walked outside to find my mother standing with her back to me, looking out towards my swing. I stopped and stood there, waiting for her to turn around or say something. When she finally spoke, it was a short sentence of cold words.

"You're such an ungrateful child," she said, without looking at me. Then, she sighed and said "I'll let them know when I'm ready to take you home. It won't be today."

She turned and brushed past me without making eye contact and walked back through the double doors. I followed her.

"Mom, please!" I cried after her. She exited through the steel door by the cafeteria without another word. I was devastated.

I took my tears to my room while the others finished their dinner. I was horrified at the thought spending an indefinite amount of time in that group home. After a short while, my sobs calmed down to sniffles and finally silence. I had to use the bathroom, so I crept out of the room down the hall. I could hear the sounds of the other teens mingling in the main room. I thought I was alone in the bathroom, but as I washed my hands, the Latina from the bed beneath mine joined me at the adjacent sink.

"You still here huh? I thought your mom came," she said with a heavy Spanish accent.

"She did," I said, holding back a sniffle. "But she left me in here."

"Damn, that's pretty cold." She stuck her hand out. "I'm Veronica."

"I'm Kisha." I shook her hand, comforted by the touch.

"I've been in here like a week and a half now. My parents kicked me out because I'm pregnant. But I ain't showing yet so don't tell nobody. I'm tryin' to figure out where I can go," she confided in me.

I was shocked that she would reveal so much information about herself at once. I needed something good to happen, and an ally in Veronica was as good as it was gonna get at that moment.

"Come on, I'll introduce you to the others," she said.

Veronica walked out to the main room with me. Everyone was gathered in the smaller conference room. Boys were on one side of the room and girls were on the other, but they were all talking and laughing together. Veronica introduced me to everyone there. One was a boy named Benjamin. He was the oldest boy, tall, with sandy-colored skin and green eyes. I figured he was biracial. His face was cute, albeit pimply, topped off by a boxy haircut. He was the clown of the group, and obviously popular.

Veronica introduced Benjamin as her 'Boo'. He smiled, draping his arm around her shoulder for a moment before the lady from the office yelled out "NO PHYSICAL CONTACT!" They backed away from each other but shared a smile that said there would be plenty more physical contact later, in the shadows. For a moment I was curious if Benjamin was the father of her child. I figured clearly not since she said no one knew she was pregnant and she had only been there a week or so.

After these introductions, I was able to relax a bit. I laughed at some of the jokes raining from Benjamin and the other boys' mouths. I sat with some of the girls and we sang pop songs to entertain ourselves. It was the early 90s. R&B was dropping bangers like babies. Xscape was crooning about kicking it, SWV was getting weak, and H-Town was knocking boots. Occasionally the boys would change song lyrics to something more explicit. The girls and I thought it was hilarious.

That was the first and last of my happy memories at the teen home for runaways. Still, I went to bed that night and prayed again to God to save me and restore my heart and home.

The next morning I awoke to a clamor in my room.

"Ewww, gross you got the pink eye!" I heard Veronica exclaim.

"That's nasty!" chimed the other Latina roommate. "She prolly got head lice too. All white people got head lice."

My white roommate who they were accusing looked mortified. But her eye was undeniably pink. Veronica had a look of disgust on her face as hurried out of the room. I didn't know what pink eye was, or that it was contagious. But I knew I didn't want it, so I quickly exited the room myself.

When I got to the bathroom, I discovered I had started my period. Blood stained my panties—the only panties I had. Horrified, I returned to ask the lady from the office to ask for help. She was surprisingly sympathetic to my situation in that instance. She found me clean panties and some pads.

"I like when ya gets your periods." She said. "It means you ain't pregnant."

I thought of Veronica as I hurried back to the bathroom to

get dressed. I put on the same donated clothes I had worn the day before. I rinsed my soiled panties as best I could, then dumped them along with my pajamas into the hamper, as I had seen the other girls do, and left the bathroom.

The rest of that Tuesday morning unfolded much like the previous one. A cold breakfast, followed by below-grade-level worksheets in a cold classroom with a cold teacher, followed by a cold lunch—a bologna sandwich that was only slightly more edible than the pizza from the day before.

After lunch, my group—Group 2—was assigned to folding laundry. I was delighted to discover that Benjamin was in Group 2. I hadn't noticed him the day before; now he stood out to me. For laundry duty, our job was to separate the boy's clothes and the girl's clothes, fold each item and leave it out on the pool table. Then, each of us would claim our items from the pool table before dinner. I was eager to locate my soiled panties before anyone else did. I was always terribly embarrassed by my period and hated leaving any evidence that I was on it. It was even worse to be on it in this place. Suddenly I heard Benjamin's voice call out.

"Good golly look at these drawers!!" He hooted and raised his hand, waving my panties through the air like a pirate's flag. "These some big ass granny drawers right here. Whose drawers are these?"

The other kids laughed. I said nothing. I just kept folding.

"Whoever they are is nasty. Look, there's a big stain in the crotch. And it's a front stain, not a back stain. Somebody on the rag," he continued.

Now several other teens hollered out in laughter. If I could see my own face, I am sure it would have been red as one of Benjamin's pimples. I forced myself to ignore the chiding. No one knew they were my panties. Benjamin soon dropped the panties and went back to his folding work. I stalled my folding long enough to be the last one at the table. Then I grabbed my panties and shoved them between my housedress pajamas, which had also been washed. I put my clothes away before heading outside to find my swing.

As dinnertime approached, I accepted that the sun would set and rise again on my group home experience. I ate the meal, which consisted of spaghetti swimming in a watery, meatless sauce, served with a mixed fruit cup. I wanted to sit with Veronica, but she had kept to herself that day. She seemed really paranoid about the pink eye situation. The girl with pink eye had left to go visit the doctor and hadn't returned. The gossip was that she probably wouldn't come back and that she definitely had lice too. I wasn't concerned about that; I had been taught that black people didn't get lice.

I made it a point to try and talk to Veronica after dinner, during our indoor free time. However, later that evening I noticed she wasn't in the main room. I figured she might not feel well, being pregnant and all. I assumed she was lying down.

I was sitting in the smaller conference room, chatting casually with a couple of the other girls, when I saw something move in the corner of my eye. I looked up and out through the glass window of the room, and saw Veronica. She was standing at the steel door. She had a look on her face that I couldn't quite read. It was a mix of fear, sadness, and determination. I gave her a puzzled look back as we locked eyes for a brief moment. I had assumed the door was locked from the inside. It wasn't. Veronica pushed the door open and took off running.

I was the sole witness. I didn't know what to say or do, so I went and found Benjamin. I told him, "I just saw Veronica run away."

"Well good for her," he said. Then he went right back to clowning with the other boys. I took it as a cue to mind my own business. But I couldn't stop thinking about Veronica running away from the runaway home.

What on earth was she running from? Or to?

I knew that Veronica had reasons for not wanting to stay there a minute longer. As I was examining my heart for her reasons for leaving, I found my own. This place was boring and depressing. There was no comfort; there was no love. It wasn't home. Was it really safe? I didn't want to find out. Desperation clicked in for me. I wanted to go home. Home to my dog. Home to my mother. Home even to my stepfather, if that's what it took to be out of this miserable place before something chased me out of its doors as well.

I went to the lady in the office.

“Can I use the phone please?” I asked.

"You’re only allowed to call your parents," she said.

"That’s fine. I want to call my mom.”

The lady nodded. I picked up the phone and dialed home.

My mom answered on the first ring. I immediately burst into tears, rambling off pleas and apologies, begging her to come and get me. I just couldn’t stay there another night.

“Put the lady on the phone.” my mother said.

I handed the phone over, and listened as the lady spoke to her.

“Yes. Ok. Goodbye,” she said, ending the call.

Less than an hour later, my mother arrived to pick me up. I was sitting in the conference room when I saw her enter through the steel doors. She made eye contact with me.

"Come on, Kisha," she said. "Let’s go.”

I went to the room I shared and stared at the empty bottom bunk beds of Veronica and the girl with pink eye. I surveyed my few belongings, tempted to abandon everything. Instead, I left the hand towel, the soap, the toothbrush and toothpaste, and the rest of the pads. I gathered up my pajamas, my stained panties, and my slippers. I put them into the bag that my mom had sent me with, along with the foam hair rollers. The last thing I put into the bag was the comb.

Then I went home.

###

My Name Is Not Kisha

So what happened to poor little Kisha?

Well, the truth is, she died.

She died in 1995, at age 14, in the final of two suicide attempts. She slit her wrist with a blade extracted from her mother's disposable razor. She bled out on the living room floor. Kisha died in a home she lived in that she hated. She shared that home with mom and a stepfather whom she hated. They were all living in San Antonio, Texas, which she hated. She killed herself because she hated herself most of all.

Two years in Texas had been rough on Kisha. For starters, Texas had stolen a promise from her—a promise of spending the 7th and 8th grade in Columbus, OH with a father and a stepmother that she loved. She only got the 7th grade. If Kisha had been mature and wise at age 12, she would have known to blame her stepmother's addiction to crack cocaine, and not the Lone Star state, for robbing her of the second year in her hometown with her father. But Kisha was neither mature nor wise, which is why she bled to death in a living room two years after moving to Texas.

Moving to Texas was only the beginning of the end for Kisha. As an only child with a mother who worked full time, Kisha spent a lot of time alone. She was grateful not to have siblings. She couldn't imagine having to share her life of scarcity with other children every day.

But a lonely life seemed like no life at all. Kisha would have loved to be around more people and to have more close friends. As a pre-teen turned teenager in Texas, Kisha would have also loved to have love. The truth is, Kisha fell in love with almost every boy she met, and almost every girl as well. The problem was none of them loved her back. Not a single one.

Rejection was a part of Kisha's everyday life. Kisha had attended eight different schools from first through eighth grade. The awkward transition into freshman year in high school was like entering the seventh circle of a hell where bullies were the demons. Sure, she'd had bullies in other grades and in other states. But in Texas her freshman year, they were the biggest, meanest, coldest bullies, building on a foundation of harassment that had been well established in the 8th grade.

After years of being ruthlessly teased, shoved around and insulted, Kisha wanted to die. She had once tried ending her life in the 8th grade. But Kisha also wasn't mature and wise enough at 13-years-old to know how to go about properly killing herself. There was no Google for these things back then. She'd drunk a seemingly toxic mixture of bleach, alcohol, and a colorful accumulation of pills known and unknown that she had gathered from the medicine cabinets at home. But the potion and pills did nothing to numb, or slow Kisha's heart. She remained utterly alive to see, and suffer, another of many miserable days.

Yet, on this fateful afternoon in Texas, at age 14, Kisha was a little wiser and a bit more mature. And, she had had it with life in Texas, for good.

She'd had it with bullies who bullied her.

She'd had it with friends who weren't really her friends.

She'd had it with a mother who was hit or miss from day to day.

She'd had it with her stepfather who was just a plain old miss.

She'd had it with being rejected.

She'd had it with being poor, black, fat, and female.

She'd had it with being herself—period.

So Kisha jerry-rigged a blade free from a disposable razor. She kissed the world goodbye before she dug the edge of the blade into her right wrist. She began an impossibly slow drag, following what she knew to be a vein. She had seen it on TV. Or maybe she read it in one of the books she could never put down. Or perhaps she saw it in a movie. Who knows? What matters is that Kisha had finally learned the right way to kill herself, without Google.

Death came swiftly, silently, and painlessly for Kisha. The mortal wound inflicted was barely 3 millimeters long.

There were only two observers to this scene of Kisha's final moments on this earth. One was her faithful dog, Windsor.

Windsor had slipped into the living room with Kisha just as she was beginning her dreadful, deadly deed. The 6-year-old Shih Tzu looked at her with eyes that said "Please don't do this. I love you." But Kisha was too far away to respond.

She had already slipped away, bleeding thick, warm blood onto the barren hardwood floors. Soon she was dead and gone.

Good thing for Windsor that there was a second observer—one that made her presence known at the very moment of Kisha's demise.

That observer was KishaLynn.

KishaLynn watched in silence. Only when she was sure that there were no signs of life remaining in the body of that lonely loser Kisha did she arise from her seat, clean up the mess, and destroy the sharp and bloody evidence.

She opted not to bury the body, because Kisha would NOT have wanted to be buried in Texas. Instead, KishaLynn took Kisha's remains and hid them where only she would ever find them again—deep inside her heart.

Then she put Windsor on a leash and took him for a walk

around the block.

In the days that followed, no one seemed to notice that Kisha was gone. No one recognized that KishaLynn was not Kisha.

So KishaLynn got funny looks when she started correcting her name to others. It didn't matter. She didn't give up. Soon enough, no one cared either way. That was fine with KishaLynn, as long as they didn't call her Kisha.

At first, life wasn't much better for KishaLynn than it was for Kisha. However, there was one significant improvement—KishaLynn was never bullied again. If you pushed KishaLynn, she pushed back. If you hit her, she hit back. She defended herself fiercely against her enemies, her friends, and her family. The 3-millimeter scar on her right wrist was the last mark of abuse she would ever bear.

She wasn't fearless—quite the opposite. KishaLynn was simply determined. She was determined to escape to a better life, as soon as possible, before the world's misery swallowed her whole, just as it had poor little Kisha—may she rest in peace.

KishaLynn's mind never wandered toward the temptation of suicide. She resolved that she would live life abundantly, and on her own terms, by any means necessary.

###

GROUNDED

I needed to get out of the hell that was Texas. So, my mother arranged to send me home to Columbus for the summer to stay with my Aunt Brenda and my cousin Nathan. I got a summer job working at COSI Museum of Science. Life was good; I finally felt at peace.

One evening my Grandma Ruth broke joyous news that my mother was leaving Tommy. She didn't say why. She only told me that my worries about him were over. It was good enough for me. Then, towards the end of the summer, my mother showed up at Aunt Brenda's doorstep driving the beat-up white car she used to share with Tommy. It was loaded with what was left of our things. Texas was over too.

My mom was only stopping through Ohio to pick up her brother and continue the drive to our new home—Boston. When my mother told me she was moving us to her hometown, I was elated. For a moment I was curious about what happened with Tommy. I also wondered what she had done with all of my things. However, I never pressed my luck with asking. I hadn't left anything, or anyone, behind of value in Texas.

I joined my mother in Boston by plane a few weeks later. Boston had a different feel to it right away. It wasn't like the smelly plains of Ohio or the greasy heats of Florida and Texas. Something about the city was crisp, fresh, and very, very dull. Boston was full of history, a subject I hadn't learned to appreciate yet. I searched for anything to be impressed by. I found it only in the mix of black and brown people from different nationalities. I also loved discovering delicious new foods like Jamaican beef patties with coco bread, West Indian roti, and New York-style pizza.

The people sounded strange to me in Boston. That was a challenge because Bostonians talk a lot, and loudly. We moved in with my mother's childhood best friend, Angela, her husband Frank, and their one-year-old daughter. Angela had grown up with my mother in Medford, MA. My early conversations with her were comical. Her Boston accent was so thick that I could barely comprehend what she was saying to me.

"My daughter is obsessed with Bonnie! It's just Bonnie Bonnie Bonnie all day around here!" Angela complained to me one day.

"What's Bonnie?" I asked. "I've never heard of it."

"What do you mean you've never heard of Bonnie? Everyone knows Bonnie! The dinosaur!" she replied.

"Oh, BARney!" I said as it clicked in my head what she was saying.

"That's what I said! Bonnie the dinosaur," Angela replied impatiently. I just laughed.

I really liked Angela. Eventually, I learned to speak her version of our English. I marveled that the people around me now spoke several languages, particularly the black people. I had grown up around Black people who only spoke English. In Boston, I met black people who spoke Spanish, French, and Creole. It was hard to know whom I could talk to at all.

I didn't have much to say in those days anyway. I was focused on my sophomore year in high school, which was fast approaching. This year would be different for me. I wouldn't be bullied or tolerate abuse from anyone. I was going to use the fresh start focus on school, make some good friends, and plan my escape to a better life in college.

I did ask one thing of my mother when we had settled in Boston—no more moves. I could not tolerate starting over anymore, as I had done virtually every year of my education before. I needed stability. I needed friends. So I implored my mother to stay put in Boston, and let me graduate with no further school changes. She agreed. Life was mine to make from there. I had this new beginning, and the next three years, to make something out of what remained of my so-called childhood.

Fall's cool breezes blew summer away. I enrolled in school. I attended Dorchester High School, one of the lowest Boston public schools at the time. It wasn't my first choice on the paper selection form. Boston English High School had a media program that appealed to me; DHS was my second choice because it offered decent career pathways that I thought would look good for college. I could make it work.

Friends were slow to come. The school wasn't at all academically rigorous, and so I was bored in class. No one at DHS seemed to care that we were there to get educated—not the students, and not the teachers. That all changed when I met Pierre. He was in my 1st-period accounting class.

One day he just turned and looked at me.

"You don't belong here," he said.

I raised my eyebrow.

Here we go. I thought.

"I believe I do," I responded. "That's what it says on my schedule."

His face broke into a charming smile, followed by a laugh.

"No, no, no," he said. Now I realized he had an accent. He was Haitian. "I meant, you do not belong here, on this side of the school."

"I don't know what you mean," I told him. It wasn't a small school building, but my high school in Texas had been four times its size. I was sure I hadn't missed anything when I toured the building myself on the first day.

"You should be on the other side, with the APS kids. The smart kids," he said, tapping his head with another gorgeous smile.

"I'm new here. No one told me about any APS. They just gave me this schedule," I said, perplexed.

"Of course! Everyone starts out over here. But then, the good kids go over to the other side of the building to learn real stuff."

I looked down at my worksheet. We were learning how to write a check in accounting class. Ironically, it was something I didn't know how to do and that I was quite curious to learn. But I also realized Pierre was referring to those career pathways that had appealed to me on the high school selection form. I remembered that my goal of escaping to a better life meant looking impressive on my college applications. I needed to be where the good kids were.

"How do you get over to the other side?" I asked.

He wiggled his eyebrows a bit. "I'll take you!" he said with exaggerated mystery in his voice.

Then we both broke into laughter and introduced ourselves. It was my first time feeling real joy since I had enrolled at that school. I had made my first friend at Dorchester High School.

True to his word, once class was dismissed, Pierre walked me over to the other side of the building. He introduced me to a tall and exuberant Italian man, with wild and wispy hair shooting out at angles around his head. I liked him immediately.

"Mr. Pisani, I'd like to introduce you to this new student, Kisha," Pierre said.

"It's KishaLynn," I corrected him.

"Sorry…KishaLynn," he said with a wink in my direction. "Anyhow, I found her wasting away over in the general population, but I figure she belongs better over here with you guys in APS."

Mr. Pisani looked at me with interest.

"Where ya from KishaLynn?" he asked.

"We just moved here from Texas. San Antonio." I answered.

"What grade are you in?"

"10th grade."

"Ahh, ok. Well APS doesn't start until 11th grade. But, let's see what English and Social Studies classes you are in. Maybe you can take them with APS teachers this year, and that will get you ready for the program next year if you're interested. Are you?"

I looked at Pierre, who stood to watch the exchange with his arms crossed and a smug grin on his face. He gave a short nod of encouragement. He looked proud—I couldn't tell if he was proud of me, or of himself.

"Yes!" I said. "Just one question—what does APS stand for?"

"Well, it's the Academy of Public Service, dear." Mr. Pisani answered with delight.

That sounded good enough for me. That would look great on my college applications. I gave Mr. Pisani a copy of my schedule, and he told me to go to the rest of my classes that day.

The following day, I received a new schedule. I still had the same math, science, musical chorus, and French classes. But I was no longer in Accounting class with Pierre. Instead, I was in Social Studies with Mr. Pisani. I was also moved to in English with Mr. Caruso, another APS teacher. This new schedule suited me much better. Mr. Pisano and Mr. Caruso, and the third APS teacher, Mr. Lucciano, quickly became my favorite teachers.

As I settled in academically, I still struggled to find my place socially. While the students in my new classes seemed friendly, Pierre was my only real friend for weeks. He was a late graduating senior—he was only enrolled for the first grading period to complete some credits. After two months, he was finished with school and I was back to being lonely.

I laid low and bored through the fall. I was delighted when snow started falling in November, heralding the start of the holiday season. I was excited about experiencing my first New

England winter. I hadn't truly experienced the season since the 7th grade when I lived with my father in Columbus. Texas had sweltering, 80-degree winter days. I liked Boston more when there was snow on the ground, even though it was freezing cold. I always preferred intense cold to intense heat. I hated sweating. In winter, I could hide my overweight body in sweaters, jackets, and wraps. Outside in a New England winter, everybody looks fat.

Angela and Frank were big on Christmas. It was their first Christmas with their daughter, so they were going all out. They introduced me to the concept of a Christmas list. I had celebrated many Christmas seasons with my mother, some merrier than others. None of them involved sitting down and distributing lists of the things we wanted. Christmas was never a huge deal to us, so I wasn't used to taking it so seriously. That said, I wasn't opposed to it. I loved Christmas.

I also loved making lists. I was always a geeky reader and writer. I made wish lists all the time in my journal—I had just never shared them with anyone, or expected to get them from anyone. I made and distributed my list with glee. It also helped me to know what other people wanted for Christmas since everyone except my mother was a stranger to me. My mom also gave me her Christmas list. She wanted a watch.

My Grandma Ruth in Ohio had sent me $100 as an early Christmas gift. The two crisp $50 bills felt like a ton of money to me at 15. I decided to spend half of the money on myself and the rest was budgeted for Christmas gifts. A few weeks before Christmas, I stuck one of the $50 bills in my boot, the other in my wallet, and went downtown to shop.

My spending money was always tight. My mother didn't take me clothes shopping very often. I was gaining weight so quickly that my clothes often didn't fit. I spent any money I had on food, clothes, music, books, and hygiene products. I could get most of those things right in the center of Boston's Downtown Crossing, and stop into my favorite store, Filene's Basement.

When I stepped into the Filene's Basement on that day, I was at the end of my shopping trip. I had bags of things I had purchased for myself throughout the day with my half of the Christmas money. I had a red shopping bag containing a new pair of winter boots in a large box, a plastic bag with two pairs of new jeans in a larger size, and a bag of hair products and cheap fragranced body sprays. I had treated myself; now I was ready to shop for others. I wanted to buy my mother's watch first and use what was left for everyone else's gifts.

It was snowing outside. I was bundled up nicely in my winter coat, scarf, earmuffs, and gloves. As I lumbered through the automatic doors of Filene's, I felt huge and heavy. But as soon as the doors closed behind me, I felt small again. I removed my earmuffs and gloves, surveying the scene. The store was packed with people, rushing from here to there, getting their holiday shopping done. Shiny white Christmas lights twinkled in a swarm overhead. The overhead sound system trilled out pop Christmas songs that cleverly replaced Jesus and Santa Claus with romantic interests. Crimson blossoms and emerald leaves of poinsettias wrapped in shimmering silver pots carved merry paths through the store. Groups of people herded along these paths to peruse the discounted wares of a field of aisles, tables, racks, and bins. All I could do was make myself a part of the crowd and go with the flow. I reared back and nudged my way into the mass of humans, using my shopping bags as a shield.

Things cleared out as I got deeper into the store and the bottleneck at the entryway was dispersed amongst the various departments available in it. I would typically head straight to the women's clothing department and dig through the few bins and racks of plus sized clothes like a truffle hog, looking for anything that would fit me, that would look good on me, and that I could afford.

However, on this trip, I veered off at the accessories department. I wasn't there to shop for me. It was time to find my mother's watch. There was a large table covered in crushed red velvet with gold trim. Scattered across the top of it, amidst miniature holly decorations, was a collection of extravagant boxed watches. I was drawn to a fancy, gold women's watch right away. It had a black face and gold dots marking the hours as gold arrows spun around it. It was perfect for my mom. I had to get it for her. But the plastic price tag had other ideas—it was marked $199.99.

I started to back away from it, but then I saw the sign at the end of the table. It read: "ALL BOXED WATCHES, 75% OFF!" For $50, I was back in play with the watch. But, buying it for my mother meant I wouldn't have money to spend on anyone else's Christmas gifts. I had already spent most of the rest of my gift money on myself.

I really liked the watch though. I just knew my mother would love it. I decided to pick the watch up and think about it. I decided that if I didn't find anything else, I would buy it for her and worry about everyone else's gifts later. I held the watch in one hand and my bags in the other as I walked around and shopped some more.

The idea to steal the watch entered my mind as I made my way towards the Men's Section to shop for Frank. A billfold caught my eye, so I examined it, moving the watch to my other hand, which was still holding my shopping bags. The wallet was too expensive, and not on sale, so I set it back down and walked away. As I was walking, I realized how easy it would be to drop the watch into my shopping bag without anyone seeing.

An instant after the realization, I had done it. I didn't even look around to see if anyone was watching. I just dropped the watch, like it was a mistake that I meant to make. I heard it land in the red bag next to the boots I had bought earlier. Then I continued on through the busy store. I knew it was wrong to steal the watch. I warmed my cold shame with the holiday spirit. I just wanted to give my mom the watch and still buy gifts for everyone else. I was wandering through the juniors' section, rationalizing my theft, when I realized it was probably a good idea for me to leave Filene's Basement.

The exit seemed an eternity away, with throngs of people and merchandise to wind through. As I started to make my way down the aisles, a tall Black woman coming in the opposite direction brushed past and bumped into me. She looked down at me, unsmiling.

"Sorry," I mumbled, even though I was sure it wasn't my fault. Then I continued ahead towards the exit. The closer I got to the door, the more crowded it became. I sighed with relief when the doors finally spit me back out into chilly open air. I watched the audacious sigh steam up in the cold and dissipate before I turned and made my way towards the train station.

The moment my foot crossed beyond the entry plaza of the store, an arm grabbed me by the elbow. I turned to see a muscular white man in a suit looking down at me with a severe frown. The strength of his grip surprised me more than the touch itself.

"I'm going to ask you to come with me," he said firmly.

"Excuse me, sir, let me go!" I shouted.

"We have you on video removing an item you did not pay for from this establishment. I'm detaining you for shoplifting. You'll need to come with me."

Then he flashed me his badge. I was sunk.

He led me around the corner. We walked through a discreet door that blended seamlessly into the facade of the building. We entered a well-lit area filled with desks and workstations. Staffers were busy working across the area. Some looked up at us as he guided me towards an office at the back of the area. A few of them gave me a *tsk tsk* look. He opened the door to the office. The black woman who had bumped into me during my bustle to get out was sitting at a desk, staring at multiple TV monitors that displayed security footage from across the store. When we entered, she turned, stood and walked over to me.

"You can set your bags down," she said. I looked down at my hand holding the bags and noticed it was shaking. I set them gently down on the floor, saying nothing.

“Ok.” She said. “We are detaining you for shoplifting. We have you on camera stealing a watch that you were observed dropping into your bag before exiting the store. You have the right to remain silent, but I am going to have to search your bags. Please take a seat on that bench.”

I sat down and watched her start going through my shopping bags. The white man who stopped me outside the store also looked on.

"Man, that’s a lot of stuff. Did you steal all of that?” he asked.

“No sir,” I said, my eyes widening in fear.

The black woman emptied the contents of the red shopping bag. The box of boots and the watch tumbled out. She picked up the watch and checked the label.

"This is ours," she said, before handing it to the white man. Then she turned her attention back to the box of boots.

"Where did you get these? Are they ours too?" she said, accusatorily.

"No ma'am," I said, my voice barely audible as my brain processed the trouble I was in. "I bought those before I came here."

"Where is your receipt?" she demanded.

I wasn't in the habit of keeping receipts, so I didn't have one to show her. She picked up the boots and looked at the label on the box.

"I'm going to call the shoe department. If these are our shoes and you don't have the receipt, we are going to have a bigger problem than we already do," she threatened.

She walked over to the desk to make a phone call. The white man stayed behind, inspecting the watch.

"Nice watch. Why did you take it without paying for it?" he asked.

"I don't know," I answered honestly. Then it occurred to me

that I still had the $50 bill in my boot.

"I have the money. I can pay for it," I said.

"Too late for that," he said. "You should have paid before you put it in your bag and walked out of the store. That's how shopping works. Anything else is shoplifting, which is a crime we take very seriously."

The black woman ended her call and came back over.

"The boots aren't ours, but the watch definitely is.," she announced. "How old are you?"

"15," I said demurely.

"Where are your parents?"

"I don't know where my mom is," I said. "Everyone went out Christmas shopping. I'm by myself."

"Well, I need to get in touch with your mother. Our policy with shoplifting is to call the police and prosecute. But, since you are a minor, I will call your mother first. If I cannot reach your mom to get down here in the next hour, I'll have to call the police. You will be arrested and taken into police custody."

My blood ran cold. The idea of being arrested was terrifying. I imagined being handcuffed and taking the third ride of my life in the back of a police car—this time to jail and not to a foster home or a group home for runaways.

She gave me a form to fill out. I wrote my name and the number to the house on it, half hoping someone would be there to answer the call, and half hoping they wouldn't. My mother was going to be absolutely furious. The thought of her wrath terrified me even more than jail. After I turned the form into the woman, she escorted me to a small holding room in the office and told me to have a seat.

"Hate to have to send a pretty thief like you to jail so close to Christmas. You better hope I reach your mom," she said somewhat sympathetically.

She turned and left, closing the door behind her. Through its window, I watched her head back to the desk before I sat down and burst into tears. I reached down into my boot and pulled out the $50.

What a selfish idiot I am!

I didn't mean to steal. I just wanted to get my mother a nice watch and buy Christmas gifts for everyone. I had never been caught doing anything wrong like this. I worried if I would have a criminal record? Would it ruin my chances of going to college? What was my mother going to do? I realized that I was burning up hot. I removed my winter coat and scarf, but that offered little relief in the small holding room where I waited.

I wasn't sure if few minutes or an hour had passed, but sooner than I was ready for it, I saw my mother's face appear in the window of the door to the room where I was being held. She looked calm. For a moment I was relieved; I said a prayer.

Please Lord, don't let her send me to jail.

After a few moments, the black woman re-entered the room holding a piece of paper.

"You're free to go. We are opting to release you to your mother instead of calling the police. You are banned from ever visiting this store. If you are seen in this store, you will be arrested immediately for trespassing. Is all of that clear?" she said, as she handed me the piece of paper to sign.

"Yes, Ma'am. Thank you," I whispered, as I commanded my quivering hands to sign the document.

"Get your things. Your mom is waiting for you outside."

I re-donned my coat, gloves, earmuffs, and scarf, feeling like I was dressing for battle. I wanted as much padding as possible on in the event my mother lost it on me. When I stepped out of the room, though, she didn't even look at me. She just started walking. I followed her, silenced by a sickening combination of guilt and terror.

When we stepped outside of the store into the winter night, my mother's friend Angela was waiting for us. No wonder my mother had arrived so quickly. I had presumed we'd take public transit home; the car we brought from Texas had been repossessed two months after we arrived in Boston.

The three of us walked silently to Angela's car and boarded. My mother still hadn't said a word, but Angela couldn't resist speaking as we all buckled up.

"How could you do this to your mother? Stealing?? It's Christmas!" she berated.

"Angela, don't." My mother said, cutting her off. "Don't speak to her."

I took a hard swallow in the back seat and wrung several fat tears from my eyes. I felt like eight fools. There was absolutely no way to explain myself. If I told my mother that the watch I had stolen was for her, I knew it would add insult to injury. I held fast to the right to remain silent that the black woman in security told me that I had.

We pulled into the driveway of Angela and Frank's house. I sat still, waiting for permission to get out alive. My mother was also still. Angela got out of the car.

I counted 10 breaths of silence before my mom spoke.

To my utter dismay, she only said three words.

"You're fucking grounded."

Her words were filled with disappointment and embarrassment. They stung like she had slapped me. I was sure a beat down was coming; but she didn't lay a hand on me. My mom exited the car and went into the house. Only when I was sure it was safe, I did the same.

There was hardly anything to ground me from since I didn't have a social life. My punishment consisted of coming straight home from school and doing nothing, which was already my daily routine. My mom and I never spoke about the incident again. Two weeks later on Christmas morning, I gave my mother a $10 watch that I bought at the local pharmacy. Everyone else got cheap gifts from the dollar store.

Even when my punishment was over, I had no friends to hang out with or to talk to on the phone. I spent my time at home, bored. Then one day, I saw Frank, Angela's husband, on his computer, logging onto something called America Online (AOL).

AOL's popularity had exploded that year. Disks and CDs for free trials of this new, dial-up Internet arrived in the mail daily. They were distributed in every store and I was very curious about it. I knew how to use a computer already. My mother had leased one from a Rent-A-Center in Texas that I used to play games and to write letters and stories. But this Internet technology was different. I had seen it on the news. It was full of information to read, pictures to look at and information to learn. Also, you could communicate, immediately, with other real live people around the world on the Internet. The concept appealed to me enormously; it sounded far better than watching television. I had to try it.

Frank was generous in allowing me to use his computer. He was a very sweet and nerdy guy. I think he appreciated my own bookish aspects. He assumed I was using the computer for noble purposes, like writing stories or letters to my friends. It had started out that way. Then one day I peeked over his shoulder while he was typing his AOL password, and memorized it. The next day, when I was home alone after school, I finally logged on.

The computer told me he had mail, then delivered me to a colorful page of portals to chat rooms on the site. I clicked one of them and watched as the computer screen started to fill with messages from strangers. I was in. I read the screen for a few minutes, before I finally I typed my first message.

ME: "Hello"

Three users responded in an instant.

USER 1: "A/S/L?"

ME: "What's that?"

USER 1: "Age/Sex/Location"

ME: "Oh. 18/Female/USA."

USER 2: "USA? This is AMERICA Online. Care to be more specific?"

USER 3: "Female? Why the male handle?"

I paused. My fingers trembled with excitement from chatting for the first time. I was so busy lying about my age that I forget I was using Frank's account, under his name. I thought for a moment, and resumed typing.

ME: "I'm from Massachusetts. Logged onto a friend's account. Sorry, I'm new to this."

A window popped up on the screen—private message.

HIM: "Are you really a female?"

ME: "Yep. All woman here."

HIM: "Is that so?"

ME: "Yep."

HIM: "Are you a good girl or a bad girl?"

ME: "Depends."

HIM: "What are you wearing?"

ME: "Clothes."

HIM: "LOL."

ME: "What's that?"

HIM: "It means laughing out loud."

ME: "Oh, did I say something funny?"

HIM: "Wanna cyber?"

My fingers backed away from the computer.

Cyber?

He was asking me to have cybersex with him. I had recently heard about cybersex in a news segment covering the dangers of the World Wide Web. I knew there were some sick people out in the world. But on the other hand, this was a stranger, he didn't know my name, my address, or anything about me beyond whatever lies I typed to him. I was too bored and too curious to say no.

ME: "Sure. First time for everything."

HIM: "Tell me what you're wearing…"

Our chat went quickly from me describing what I thought was a sexy outfit, to his virtual fingers all over and then inside my Internet body. I scraped the details of what I was doing to him from pornographic scenes I had studied from my father's hidden stash over visits to Columbus, serving up a virtual hand job and writing out a blowjob so descriptive that even I was impressed.

ME: "I swallow your cock whole, milking the tip with the back of my throat until you come."

HIM: "*groan*"

To me, this was great cybersex. I was having fun. I could tell he was too, despite my unconfirmed age and gender. I wasn't touching myself, but I did feel a rush that was new to me. It felt like the most invigorating thing I'd done in my whole life. When it was time to end our chat session, he asked if we could chat again. I reminded him that I relied on a friend's account.

HIM: "Tell me when you'll be on again, and I'll meet you."

ME: "I'll try to log-in again tomorrow at the same time."

HIM: "Hey what's your name?"

I paused on the keys for a moment, choosing a name. It was an easy decision.

ME: "Lynn. Yours."

HIM: "Bobby."

ME: "OK Bobby. Nice to meet you."

BOBBY: "You too Lynn. TTYL"

ME: "Ummm, is that talk to you later?"

BOBBY: "LOL yep."

ME: "LOL."

*****END CHAT*****

Bobby and I chatted hot and heavy for the next two weeks, whenever we could manage to be logged on at the same time. Our chats always included cybersex, but I did manage to learn a little about him. He was a Black divorcee from Chicago. He worked at a law firm, but he wasn't a lawyer. His offline hobbies were raising Rottweiler dogs and playing basketball. But he spent most of his free time in chat rooms on AOL.

I avoided giving him many details about myself, and he didn't seem to mind. Then suddenly, he wanted more.

BOBBY: "Can I call you?"

I panicked.

ME: "Why do you want to call me?"

BOBBY: "You bring me so much pleasure online. I want to hear your voice. You can call me if you don't want to give me your number."

ME: "It's a long distance call. That costs money."

BOBBY: "LOL I have a job. I can pay. Give me your number, and I'll call you."

I was trapped. I didn't want to stop chatting with Bobby. I was afraid if I didn't agree to at least one phone call then he would think I was a guy after all. I realized I was afraid to lose him. I didn't have anything else this exciting happening in my life.

ME: "OK. I'll give you the number where I am right now. But I don't live here, so please don't ever use this number at any other time."

BOBBY: "OK, what is it?"

I took a deep breath and typed out Frank and Angela's telephone number. I hesitated for just a second before sending.

ME: 617-###-####.

BOBBY: "Cool. Let me log off. I'll call in a few minutes."

*****END CHAT*****

I paced the room anxiously with the phone handset in my hands. Bobby was getting ready to call me. This was going beyond typing dirty words now. A phone call was another level. I watched the clock while my mind raced. Had it been three minutes yet? Had he changed his mind? Should I log back on and see if he's there?

The phone rang. It sounded louder than I expected and I jumped, startled at the sound. I collected myself, cleared my throat, and then answered the phone with my most grown-sounding voice.

"Hello?"

"Hey," he said.

Bobby's voice was surprisingly deep. It turned me on right away. I thought about his naughty words on the screen. I wondered if I'd be hearing his fantastic voice say any of those words on this call.

"See, told you I was all woman," I said huskily.

"Yep, yep you are. Although I figured that out pretty quickly. A man couldn't write sex like that," he said.

"Thanks, I think," I said with a chuckle. "And thanks for picking up the cost of the call."

"No problem. Now, make it worth my while. Tell me what you're wearing," he murmured.

Those were his keywords for cybersex. Now, he wanted phone sex. I couldn't say no; I didn't want to.

"Nothing. I didn't want anything to get in your way, baby. You got something for me?" I responded.

"Oh yeah," I heard him breathe heavily into the phone. "I got something nice and hard for you."

"Well come and give it to me, baby. I want it all," I continued.

As we went back and forth, I had to cover the mouthpiece of the phone to muffle the sounds of my laughing as he moaned through our phone call. He was obviously masturbating. Bobby wasn't even talking anymore-. I could hear him sucking air through his teeth and moaning it out while I purred back in his ear, pretending to touch myself. Then I heard him take a sharp breath.

"Oh shit!" he exclaimed as he exhaled a whoosh of air into my ear, orgasming on the other end of the line.

"Mmm, that was nice, baby," I rasped.

"Mmm hmm," he mumbled, "real nice."

"Listen, I gotta go now. But thanks for calling me," I closed hastily.

"OK, catch you later," he said without complaint.

I hung up the phone and squealed. I made a man come!! Over the phone! It was the closest thing I'd had to real sex thus far. I felt like I had lost my virginity without actually having sex. I felt a little dirty, but my purity was still intact. I was safe, and no harm had been done. I couldn't wait to log back on to AOL the next day and chat with him again.

But that didn't happen. Instead, that night my mother called me into the kitchen where she was sitting with Frank and Angela. I knew it was trouble for me by the look on her face, but I couldn't tell what I had done wrong yet.

"Have you been using my computer lately?" Frank asked quietly.

"Yes," I said, feeling a sense of dread grow deep inside my stomach.

"Have you been going online on my America Online account?" he asked.

My knees started to give, but I held my ground.

"A little," I said, lowering my eyes. I knew I was busted, but I didn't know how busted I was yet. Had they seen my chats with Bobby? Did they know about the earlier phone call?

Frank picked up a stack of papers from the table. "I would say this is quite a bit more than a little." He showed me the papers, which looked like a phone bill except that instead of phone numbers it had his AOL username, with minutes and prices next to. It was the AOL bill. I had no idea that using America Online cost $3 an hour, or five cents a minute! I had been secretly chatting with Bobby for 1-2 hours per day for the past month. The amount due was over $100.

My mother and Angela seemed furious, but Frank was very calm.

"Frank, I'm sorry. I had no idea that there were fees for using the Internet on the computer." I said penitently.

"Yep. There are. It's not entirely your fault though. I shouldn't have allowed you to use the computer unmonitored. But, you should have asked first. I spoke with your mom and we've agreed that, unfortunately, I have to prohibit you from using my computer anymore. Let's all take this as a lesson learned," he said.

"I understand," I said shamefully, still looking at my feet, mostly to avoid my mother's eyes.

"I'll pay the bill, but we can work out a way to pay back the money you ran up," Frank said gently.

"Yes, you will," my mother added, with a threat in her voice.

He never questioned how I had gotten his password to login to AOL. He never mentioned if he had been able to see any of my chat logs. The issue died right there, and so did my access to Bobby. For the time being.

In the summer after my sophomore year ended, I enrolled in an early college at UMass Boston. The program paid at-risk high school students minimum wage to take college-level courses, with the goal of building life skills and preparing us for college. Students in the program received UMass Boston email addresses.

I was finally given access to the Internet again, for free and in private, from the UMass computer lab. The minute I was logged on, I emailed Bobby at his AOL address.

SUBJECT LINE: Blast From The Past

MESSAGE:

"Hey, baby. Remember me? It's been a long time. I miss you. Write me back if you get this. -Lynn"

Much to my surprise, he wrote me back.

SUBJECT LINE: RE: Blast From The Past

MESSAGE:

"Hey. Where have you been? It's been forever. I've missed you too, but I'm still around. LOL".-Bobby

I yelped in celebration in the computer lab, prompting disapproving looks from actual UMass Boston students whose heads popped up to see what the noise was. I had Bobby back, and I wasn't going to lose him again. I wrote back, picking up my lies where they had left off so many months before. I told him t that I'd recently started college and could only email him twice a week when I was in the campus computer lab. That was enough to keep us connected until I had my own computer.

My mother and I moved into our own place, right next to my high school. I had my own room again. As an added bonus, my mother allowed me to have my own phone line installed. I paid the bill with money I earned from the college program. I was desperate for a computer, but didn't earn enough to buy one. However, my high school science teacher, Mr. Grant, showed me how to build myself a computer out of a technology boneyard that he maintained in the school basement.

I took me three trips over as many days to carry all of the computer pieces home and then set it up the way Mr. Grant had demonstrated at the school. This computer was old and clunky. It only no mouse. The monitor didn't even display images; everything on it was text-based, manipulated by the keyboard. But all that mattered to me is that it had a modem. I asked Mr. Grant if he could help me get online using my phone line at home. He showed me how to dial up the Internet for free by accessing the college network.

The process took a few minutes of typing green text on the dusty black monitor screen. Once the correct keystrokes were entered, the modem would connect the phone line, dial the number and give me that infamous squeal of freedom and excitement as I connected to the rest of the world. Of course, there was no AOL on this computer. But, I was able to access my UMASS-Boston email to resume communications with Bobby. I also discovered the Alamak website, which had chat rooms similar to AOL. I could access these rooms from my ancient computer. Now I had the virtual world at my fingertips.

However, my romantic Internet reunion with Bobby was short-lived. He preferred to use AOL for Internet chatting. I didn't have access to AOL, so we could only email each other online. Bobby and I relied primarily on phone calls to stay in touch. Soon the phone bills got to be too much for him. I started spending most of the little money I made from my work internships on phone cards to call him.

I could tell Bobby was getting bored. One night he insisted on having another woman join us for a three-way phone sex call. I didn't really want to share him. But, I was curious to know what talking to a woman would be like, so I agreed.

As we began the call, at first, it was exciting to be having phone sex with a Bobby and another girl at the same time. I felt like I was joining a virtual threesome! Then I noticed that they were really only speaking to each other on the call. So, I opted to listen in while I assessed the best way to approach the conversation.

Just as things were starting to heat up on the call, I was suddenly disconnected. I waited for minutes, then hours for them to call me back before I realized it wasn't going to happen. They had just hung up on me.

An email from Bobby the next day disconnected me for good.

SUBJECT LINE: [NO SUBJECT]

MESSAGE:

"Sorry. It's been real.-Bobby."

###

GINA

I lost my virginity to a boy from school in 1997, at age 16. It was more of an experiment than an act of rebellion. I was I was feeling curiously attracted to girls, and worried that I might be gay. But as a Christian, I knew I couldn't cross that line. So, attempting to normalize myself, I found a willing boy from school and had unremarkable sex with him 11 times before I got bored and we stopped. The attraction to women was still there. I continued to wonder what that meant for my sexuality.

I was fortunate enough to have unfettered access to the Internet at home. I had my own phone line in my bedroom where I could dial up, uninterrupted, day and night. My mom had no idea of what I was being exposed to in Internet chat rooms. LynnBeauty97 was free to live a second life in chats and private messages with strangers.

I loved how the Internet allowed me to be who I wished I could be in real life. LynnBeauty97, aka "Lynn," could do the things I wished I could do if God was not watching. And boy, did Lynn do things—with men and women—online. Friendly chats soon became cybersex, where I learned to write sex well. Cybersex would evolve into phone sex, where I learned how to sound very grown on the phone. But it wasn't an adequate substitute for what I needed. It was time to put God's forgiveness to the test, and craft a new experiment.

So I placed an ad on the Classifeds2000 website. The headline was:

**Single Black Virgo, 18, BBW,
Seeking First Time With A Woman**

That same night, Gina replied. She felt drawn to my ad because she was a Cancer—a "Moonchild". Apparently our signs were compatible. She had been with a woman before and wanted to try it again. She had just turned 30 and she had a boyfriend named George. She was my first and only reply. I was beyond excited.

I held my breath while I waited about 20 seconds for her attached picture to load. Line by line, pixel by pixel, an image emerged of a beautiful, white, redheaded, emerald-eyed woman. I finally exhaled as I replied to her message.

We arranged a meet up at a restaurant. I wasn't comfortable going directly to Gina's house. This was my first time meeting a person off of the Internet. I felt I needed to take precautions.

I grew anxious as I walked up to the restaurant. Could I pass as an 18-year-old, knowing full well that I was only 16? Was I going to be beautiful enough? Charming enough?

She showed up 30 minutes late. I had a curfew so I knew

we'd have to keep our time together short. When she walked up to the table, she gave me a big smile. My concerns about her attraction to me melted away. She wrapped me in a hug. As I felt her for the first time, I knew that this was something I wanted, more than anything now.

Our conversation was easy and filled with laughter. I ordered clam chowder. It was all I could afford.

"That's appropriate for this particular occasion," Gina joked with a twinkle in her eye.

I laughed even though I didn't get it. As we paid the bill, she asked if she could see me again. I said yes and smiled. She smiled back. This time, we both got it. We arranged another meet up for the following weekend. We would be alone. This time, I would go to her. All the way to her.

The day finally came. My mom knew I was taking the SAT, so she had no questions when I told her I'd be gone for most of the day. It was a terrible idea to actually take the SAT exam before this very important date. I was grateful I would get to retake it during my senior year. I just couldn't concentrate as I penciled in the answer bubbles on the excruciating four-hour exam. When the test came to an end, I couldn't care less about my scores. I left the testing center ready to make a new beginning.

I asked Gina to pick me up at a trolley station off Boston's Red Line. This time, she arrived right on schedule. I tried my best to look casual as I hopped into her car. I carried with me a small bag that contained my wallet, my SAT test materials, and a white lace negligee that I had borrowed from my mother's drawer that morning. We were mostly silent for the short ride to her house.

She welcomed me inside her place with a flourish of her hand. I took a quick look around cozy space while trying to calm my nerves. My heart pounded in my throat. Gina looked like she might devour me.

Are we really going to do this?

We sat on a love seat in a darkened den, and she put on a movie called Set It Off. It was an appropriate choice—a film about four black women, one of them a lesbian, played by Queen Latifah, one of my celebrity crushes. We watched the film comfortably together, in a silence that only increased the intensity of the moment. Then a sex scene with Jada Pinkett came on, and I could feel the temperature in the room plink up a couple of degrees. She asked if she could hold my hand. I opened mine to hers. I knew that it was already happening. After the sex scene was over, she leaned in close to whisper in my ear.

"May I kiss you?" she asked.

"Yes," I answered.

The first time my lips touched her, I felt a flash of power that shocked me from head to toe. I had never felt so turned on by a kiss before. Then I began to taste her. Her lips were flavored with a fruity balm. Her teeth had a metallic tinge when my tongue brushed across them. Her saliva had such a sweet tanginess to it that I wanted to shove my fingers in her mouth and lick them clean. Everything about her was delicious and right. This was sexual attraction. It was a feeling I had only imagined before.

When the kiss ended, she invited me to her bedroom. I somehow agreed while struggling to bring my senses back together from the kiss.

"May I use the restroom first?" I asked. I needed a moment to prepare myself.

She pointed me to the bathroom, then to the bedroom door just across from it.

"Meet me in there when you are ready," she said suggestively.

I grabbed my bag and shut myself into the bathroom. I leaned my back against the door, taking a few moments to breathe deeply. Then, I looked at my face in the mirror. It was all flushed with lust. The reality of impending sex deepened the red in my cheeks. My hazel-brown eyes had darkened into a wicked cinnamon shade. I couldn't even think about God. I quickly changed out of my clothes and them into my bag. I was ready. I left the bathroom and entered Gina's bedroom.

She was lain naked as sin, spread out on the bed.

There I stood in my mother's nightgown, which I felt both foolish and fortunate for wearing. I had made my entrance, and so had she. It was time to get to it.

I dropped my bag and climbed on the bed. We locked ourselves into a tangle of long kisses. I held Gina awkwardly at first, like I was afraid I would break her. But as I got more comfortable, I allowed my hands to wander. I had never touched a woman's breasts before. I cupped hers like palm fruits. Her nipples got hard, and that surprised me. My nipples didn't do that. I'm pretty sure that meant she liked it.

In my mind, there was one thing that would make this experience with a woman the real deal, and not just a make-out session. I had to go down on her.

I was scared that something would happen to interrupt the moment before the deed was thoroughly done, so I made my way down her body. She laid back, and her legs fell open. The lips of her pussy parted before me, covered in fiery, red hairs. I was awestruck. It stared back at me with an expression that I studied for a few moments. Then, I planted my face right into the center of it.

I was surprised by her taste—it was clean and just a bit salty. I didn't know what to expect, but it wasn't that. My tongue lapped its way around her silky folds. She moaned in pleasure.

Oh shit! I'm doing this!

I tried wiggling my face around the way I had seen done in Internet porn. She went still and silent. I hadn't even discovered my own clitoris yet; I licked around searching for hers. When her moaning started again, I knew I had found it. I flashed back to the virtual fantasies I had shared online with women. They inspired me to get bold and throw my fingers into the action. I finger-fucked her aggressively.

I must have done it too hard, because I looked down and saw blood on my fingers. It wasn't a lot of blood, but enough to make me pull my mouth away. I was paranoid about STDs. I realized that I had been meticulous about safe sex when I lost my virginity. Now I was openly exchanging bodily fluids with a stranger with no protection. I didn't even know what proper protection would be in this scenario. I realized my fingers were still inside of her, and I pulled them out.

She rolled over and pushed me back against the pillows.

"It's your turn," she said with a warm smile. As she climbed on top of me, I could feel myself clamming up. I wasn't sure I was ready to receive oral sex. I felt self-conscious and uncomfortable with my body. The idea of having someone tasting me down there almost repulsed me. But I couldn't very well back out now. I figured that I might as well take this ride all the way home.

Her lips were just about to touch mine down there when I heard a door shut outside the bedroom. She jerked her head up, looking over her shoulder.

"That's George," she said.

I could not sit up in the bed fast enough.

"Your boyfriend? Oh my God!" I whispered.

"Calm down," she said. "He knows you're here."

That only made me freak out more. Suddenly I felt very unsafe.

"You said we'd be alone," I said, sounding alarmed.

"He's just here early. But it's ok. You can leave if you'd like," Gina said.

"Yes I would like to leave," I said, already climbing out of the bed to reach for my clothes. "Is George going to trip that I'm in here with you?"

"Oh no," she said. "He knows all about this and you." She began dressing like it was no big deal.

I felt embarrassed and a little upset. I wasn't prepared to meet Gina's boyfriend. Now I had no choice.

We were fully dressed when she opened the bedroom door. There stood the most unattractive white guy I'd ever seen. I struggled to hide my look of disapproval. He was fatter than me and shorter than both Gina and I. He was dressed lazily, in sweatpants and a T-shirt. His beady eyes gazed out as us behind thick-rimmed glasses. My feeling of danger dispersed. I was quite confident that I could kick George's ass in a struggle if he tried to bust a move. I couldn't believe this beast, who somehow managed to be huge and small at the same time, was this gorgeous woman's boyfriend. He looked at me, then Gina, with a knowing smile on his face. That smile pissed me off.

"You're here early," she said.

"Yeah, sorry babe," he replied.

"This is Lynn," she introduced us.

"Nice to meet you," I said, even though it wasn't.

He gave me a nod. I intentionally did not reach to shake George's hand; I didn't move at all.

The three of us stood in awkward silence. She could see that I was uncomfortable. She grabbed her keys from the counter.

"I'm gonna take her back," she told him, bending down a bit to kiss him on the cheek. At that moment, I was glad that she hadn't gone down on me. I didn't want him to know what my pussy smelled like. We departed.

I breathed a heavy sigh of relief when we were out of the house and I was buckled into my seat in her car.

"Sorry about that," she said. "He wasn't supposed to come by for another hour or so."

"It's ok. Thanks for giving me a ride back," I felt that Gina's apology was sincere. It comforted me.

"I had a good time," she said quietly.

"So did I," I responded. Then I lost myself in silent thoughts for the rest of the ride. When we arrived at the trolley station, I waved goodbye, then exited Gina's car feeling like a woman.

I had 16 stops on the Red Line from Alewife to Ashmont to process the reality of the experience. I breathed in memories of our first kiss...the sight of her naked...the way she tasted. I knew I wanted more, even if it made me a...

Oh, God…

The shame hit me as I was walking up the street to my house. I had definitely crossed the line. What about God? Would He punish me for this?

My mother was cooking in the kitchen when I walked in, just before dark.

"How was the SAT?" she asked.

"Long," I answered with a truthful sigh.

"Well, I've got some news," she said, turning from her task of stirring.

We locked eyes. I wondered if somehow she knew.

"What's wrong?" I asked. For a brief moment, I thought about the blood on my hands.

"Grandma Ruth died a few hours ago," she said.

I was inconsolable.

Less than 48 hours after I lowered myself onto Gina's pink pearl, I watched my beloved Grandma Ruth's body as it was lowered into the ground in a pearl-pink casket. Guilt crushed my heart. I was certain that this was God's punishment for succumbing to my sinful homosexual desires. Grandma Ruth's death was a sudden tragedy to me. I didn't even know she was ill. I later learned that she had insisted on my ignorance of her deteriorating condition. That didn't help numb the pain of her loss.

A week after I returned from my Grandma Ruth's funeral in Columbus, I got an email from Gina. It said that that she had decided not to pursue her interest in women further. She revealed that she had broken up with George and was going to focus on herself. I didn't even respond to the email. I deleted it, and her, from my inbox and life, never to be seen or heard from again. Grandma Ruth's death had scared me straight.

I continued to grieve the loss well into the start of my senior year in high school. Still, I found the motivation to focus on college applications. I applied to nine schools, mostly in Chicago and Ohio. Since I knew it was up to me to pay for college, I also completed every scholarship application I could get my hands on.

Then, one Friday in January, just as a quiet, light snow had begun falling in Boston, I rounded the corner of our street walking home from school and saw a bunch of our stuff sitting out on the sidewalk. I broke into a run towards the house, believing we were being robbed. I stopped short when I saw my mother exiting the front door with a box in her hands. Her face was ashen, her eyes were swollen from tears. She didn't even look at me.

"We're being evicted," she said.

I had no clear idea of why we were being evicted. We had just moved in to that house. I didn't know where we were going to go, or what we were going to do. Suddenly we were homeless.

My mom found a space for us to stay, doubled-up with a new friend of hers who lived right behind the house we were kicked out of. The friend, Audrey, was mentally disabled, so she didn't work. She was a pottery artist and a self-professed weed addict. Regardless of how bizarre she was, we were grateful that she opened her home to us. She even helped us move our things into her home from the sidewalk.

Her house was on the verge of being condemned. Filth accumulated everywhere the eye looked. Every inch of it was crammed with items that seemed useless and dangerous. Stacks of newspapers were heaped in corners. A piano with only six surviving keys leaned against the staircase in the hallway at the entry. Months worth of mail piled high on a shelf behind the door. Even the walls and ceiling were dirty. When I took a shower in her bathroom, I would feel dirtier stepping out of it than I did getting in. At night, I listened to mice congregating in the walls of my attic bedroom. They terrified me. It was a nightmare. But it was better than a winter night on the freezing streets of Boston. Clearly, my mother had nowhere better for us to go. So I repressed my disgust and swallowed my complaints. I was tempted to wonder why life offered me nothing but challenges. Then, I would remind myself that God's grace was still shining on me. Once I graduated from high school and went to college, it would be better.

All I had to do was survive my circumstances long enough to make it there.

###

This Nigga-Part 1

My hard work had paid off; I had flourished at Dorchester High School. It was my senior year, and my eyes were on the prize. College acceptance letters began to find their way into the mess that convened at the door of the dilapidated shelter provided by mom's friend Audrey. Audrey had taken us in when we were evicted that winter. We were living in squalor, but I clung to the hope of imminent freedom after graduation.

I decided to attend Spelman College. Scholarship awards started pouring in by early spring. When a life-changing benefactor came forward with an offer to fund my college education in its entirety, I knew my fate was sealed. For once in my life, that was a good thing. It made the dark, dirty walls of Audrey's house feel brighter at moments.

I was at the top of my school's senior class of 1998, a captain on the cheerleading squad, as well as senior class president. It would be easy to think I was finally happy. But there was a problem.

No one would take me to prom. No one. Everyone I asked said no. I gave up after the third guy laughed in my face. I relegated myself to not going to prom.

I wasn't expecting my mother to ask about prom, but she surprised me.

"Hey, isn't prom season coming up?" she asked one evening while we sat at a rickety table in Audrey's kitchen eating dinner.

"Yeah. It's coming up," I answered with a shrug.

"Who are you going with?"

"I'm actually not going to prom this year."

"What? It's your senior year! Why wouldn't you go to prom?"

"I can't find a date. I already went to junior prom last year without a date, and it was lame. Besides, I'm senior class president. We're planning this prom, and trust me, it's nothing to be excited about. There's no budget, and the whole thing is kind of a disaster!"

It was the most I had opened up to my mother about my school life in a while, and the first time she seemed genuinely interested. I was a bit suspicious as to why she took such an interest in my senior prom. She had barely congratulated me on my college and scholarship success. Those were much more significant than prom. What was so special about a school dance?

"You have to go to your senior prom. Let's just find you a date!" my mom said intently.

"Good luck with that. I'd really rather just skip it. Why does it matter to you anyway?" I asked.

"Well," my mom said with a reflective with pause, "I didn't get to go to my senior prom because I was pregnant with you."

There it was.

"I'd really like to see if we can get you to prom. I'm sure I know someone who can take you," my mom said.

"I know someone," Audrey said, appearing in the kitchen as if on cue. She always had impeccable timing with her comings and goings in the house. "You are a smart, beautiful girl. Listen to your mom. Go to prom. I have a date for you."

"What date could you possibly have in mind for me?" I asked.

"My son has a friend. Remember, you met him a couple of weeks ago when the house flooded," she reminded.

It was actually hard to forget. I had come home from work one evening to find a vacuum hose snaking up the stairs to the house. I followed it inside and looked up to see a leaking swell of water damage spread across the ceiling, raining down into a muddy puddle on the ground floor. I rushed up the stairs to see the source of the flooding. At the top of the steps, holding the tip of the vacuum that had greeted me outside, was This Nigga.

He was so strikingly handsome that all thoughts about the

water damage and flood paused for a moment as we locked gazes on each other. His eyes were the same hazel color as mine. Perhaps they were a little greener. Freckles splashed across his khaki-colored skin. He was tall, bald, and built. He was fine as hell—an absolute Adonis to my eyes.

This Nigga spoke first.

"What do you get when a cat meets a waterbed?" he had asked. Somehow his voice sounded even better than he looked. I felt tingles that a man had never generated in me.

I knew his question was bait, and yet I still took it. I couldn't resist.

"One wet pussy," I answered. We both laughed in a way that was far too familiar for two strangers.

It turned out that Audrey's cat, Smokey, had clawed through her king-sized water mattress, causing the flood on the second floor. I was grateful that my room was in the attic on the third level and very glad only to be catching the aftermath of the event. I mentally added this catastrophe to the list of things that made Audrey's house anything but an adequate home.

I knew for a fact that This Nigga was 20 years older than me, because later that same night of the flood, I met him outside as he was leaving.

"How old are you?" I asked.

“37 years young,” he answered, “I grew up with Audrey’s son. He’s my best friend.”

“Wow. You don’t look 37,” I replied. He was actually two years older than my mother.

“It’s because I use Oil of Olay every day darling,” he said. This Nigga smiled with dimples I could make out even in the dark. “What, if I may ask of a beautiful young lady, is your age?”

He knew Audrey, so there was no point in lying to him.

“I’m 17,” I answered.

He sucked in his teeth and jumped back like I had scalded him with hot oil.

“Yikes. You’re jailbait,” he claimed.

"Good thing your best friend is a cop, huh?" I answered. I was used to this level of banter behind a keyboard, chatting online. Something about This Nigga had it flowing naturally face-to-face.

“Touché,” was all he said, before bidding me a farewell that felt fond in my wildest fantasy.

I hadn’t thought about This Nigga since that night, but the second Audrey mentioned him, I couldn’t help but perk up a bit. I rose from the table to clear my dishes.

“Oh, yeah I remember him. But isn’t he much older than

me?" I asked.

“He looks much younger!” my mother chimed in.

I mulled it over. This Nigga was very attractive. He was far out of my league regardless of age.

“What makes you think he’ll be my prom date?” I asked them both.

“He won’t have a choice,” Audrey answered. “Nor will he want one,” she added.

I was incredulous at the whole conversation but intrigued by the possibility of prom night with someone so gorgeous, even if he was on loan.

“If he says yes, I guess I’ll consider it,” I decided. They were both visibly pleased.

“You know, I didn’t get to go to my prom either,” Audrey said. Neither my mom nor I asked why.

I figured I would wait for my mom and Audrey to give me the sad news that This Nigga had declined. Instead, the next night my phone upstairs rang. That was unusual because I only used my phone line to connect to the Internet. No one called me unless it was pre-arranged.

I felt the tingles again as soon as I heard his voice on the line. This Nigga needed no introduction.

"Hello, Beautiful. I am calling to ask for the honor of accompanying you to your prom," he said.

I was instantly dazed. I don't expect This Nigga to say yes. Or to contact me directly.

"Hello? Are you there?" he asked.

"Yes!" I stammered.

"Yes, you're there, or yes, I can be your prom date."

"Yes! Ummm….yes...to both." I struggled to calm myself down. I picked the worst time to act like a 17-year-old.

"Excellent!" he said, in the style of Montgomery Burns from The Simpsons. "How about I come by tomorrow, and you can give me all the details?"

"Perfect!" I said, "I'll be here. You know the address." I joked.

"That I do. Until soon, Beautiful." I melted when he called me beautiful. It hadn't slipped past me that he'd said it twice.

I hung up the phone with a squeal before rushing downstairs to tell mom and Audrey what they clearly already knew.

True to his word, This Nigga showed up the next night to meet with my mother, Audrey, and I to discuss prom logistics. Just like that, I went from not going to prom, to planning the prom night of my dreams, complete with limo, flowers, and a real-life Prince Charming on my arm. Adding to my luck, the same generous benefactor who was funding my full-ride college scholarship took me shopping and gifted me with an elegant prom dress and makeup.

Every girl deserves to feel the way I felt when prom night finally came. I donned my eggplant purple lace and silk prom dress and shoes, which had cost a small fortune at Saks Fifth Avenue. My mother curled and pinned my hair up. I did my own makeup using the gifted products.

At 5:30 PM on prom night, This Nigga rolled up fresh and clean in a white stretch limousine. He was wearing a black tux, Stacy Adams black & white shoes. He handed me a gorgeous purple and white corsage to match my dress. My mom and Audrey pinned it on and gushed over me. They took photos before they released me into the night with This Nigga.

My senior prom night was magical. This Nigga was a perfect date in every sense of the word. I had the unique experience of watching heads turn as I strolled past my classmates with him walking into the hotel. The girls stared at him as helplessly as I had, but he kept his eyes and attention on me, putting his arm around my waist and holding me proudly at his side the way I had always dreamed someone would one day hold me. He held open doors, carried my small purse, and doted over me like the experience was real. I had to keep reminding myself that it wasn't.

I lived the fantasy for four hours. This Nigga wasn't much of a dancer, but he did hold me close and sway through every slow song. In his arms, I sighed as Savannah Jackson did in Terry McMillian's "Waiting to Exhale." As the end of the night approached, I felt like Cinderella without a glass slipper.

I was depressed during the limo ride home. To hide my sadness, I pretended to fall asleep during the trip, resting my head against This Nigga's chest. He wrapped his arm around me. I appreciated it. He didn't have to pretend anymore since the night was now over. But I was glad he stayed in character, holding me while I listened to his heartbeat thunder in his chest.

When the limo pulled up to Audrey's house, I expressed my gratitude and wished out loud that the night didn't have to end. This Nigga had been such a gentleman.

"Thanks for playing make-believe with me," I said, stifling a quiver of remorse in my voice.

"You must be tired. You slept the ride home. Get some rest. Good night, Beautiful," he responded.

The warm hug he had wrapped me in lingered for a moment. I thought he was doing me a favor.

The following morning I was startled awake by the jangle of my phone ringing. I slapped my hand around the headboard blindly, grabbing the receiver and pulling it under the covers with me.

"Hello?" I answered, my voice still groggy with sleep.

"I'm sorry."

It was This Nigga! I woke up immediately.

"For what?" I asked.

"I failed you as a prom date," he continued.

"How's that?"

"I didn't feed you afterward."

"Is that a thing?" I had no expectations of a meal. He had already paid for our tickets, a tux, flowers, and the limo.

"It should be, for any man who is worth your time."

I thought the time of my tingling from This Nigga's words had passed. I was wrong.

"Ok so, I guess you owe me a meal then." I'd have given anything to spend another moment with him, so I opted out of subtlety, especially since he had called me.

"How about breakfast?" he asked.

"Today?" I couldn't believe it.

"Yeah, if you want. I can be there in a few minutes to pick you up. That is if you forgive me for failing you last night."

"Consider yourself forgiven. I'll be ready in 30 minutes."

I hung up the phone, but this time I had to silence my squeal.

I wasn't sure my mom would be as approving of me seeing This Nigga outside of prom.

Check yourself, KishaLynn. Remember, This Nigga is more than twice your age.

All the warnings in the world couldn't have helped me. When This Nigga pulled up in a boxy, blue Ford Thunderbird, I knew the moment I climbed in that I would go wherever this ride took me.

This Nigga took me to his house. Actually, it was his mother's house. He lived there with his parents and his grandmother. The car also belonged to his mother. His room was in the basement of the home. I ignored how pathetic that fact was. His parents were out of town for the weekend, so we had the place to ourselves.

"What happened to breakfast?" I asked as we entered, layering my voice with fabricated suspicion.

"I'm on the redemption path, so I decided to step my game up and cook for you," he said.

He led me into the kitchen where he showed off a spread of eggs, sausage, and canned biscuits all prepped out for cooking on the counter.

"Wow. I'm impressed!" I said.

"I'm just getting started, Beautiful," he said with a dazzling smile. I hoped he was right, even if I didn't dare pray to make it so.

"Here, let me show you around," he offered.

I assessed my surroundings. There wasn't much to see on this main level of the single-family house. The front door had opened into a dining/living room combo that was stuffed with old-fashioned furniture. The kitchen was just off to the side, attached to a hallway that led to some bedrooms and a bathroom. Across that hallway was a small staircase that led downstairs to the basement. I followed him down there, fully aware of the rabbit hole I was entering.

This Nigga didn't even have the whole basement to himself. The majority of the space contained even older furniture than the upstairs, surrounded by storage boxes. There was a small bathroom with a stand-up shower in it to the right of the staircase. The basement level had its entry door along the back wall. To the right of that door was a smaller room, This Nigga's room.

Stepping into his room, things immediately felt more intimate. I scanned the walls, which were covered with airplane paraphernalia, cartoon stickers, and comic posters. There was a large mirror hanging above the dresser, and a TV and VCR sat on top of it. His bed was on the opposite wall, with only about three feet of clearance between it and the dresser. Stacks of VHS tapes were piled on the floor, which made the space even tighter. At the foot of his bed, to the left of the bedroom door, was a computer surrounded by PC games.

"Do you go online?" I asked, curious if he too had an Internet persona.

"No. That computer is ancient. I basically just use it to play Solitaire," he said, shrugging.

"Oh," was all I could say.

It occurred to me that this wasn't at all how I imagined a man's room to look. I felt like I was in a teenager's boy cave.

Thoughts of teenage anything vanished when This Nigga turned his attention to me directly.

"You know, there was something else I screwed up last night," he said, staring into me with so much intensity that I felt the room shrink to half its size half. I didn't look away. I couldn't. The tingles were on overload. This time I strongly suspected that the itch that started in my loins the night that Smokey flooded the house was about to be scratched.

He stepped closer to me. I was unable to resist the surge of passion within me, so I took a step closer too. Our bodies met and our lips met for the kiss I had been living for. This kiss would have raised me from the dead if every fiber of my being wasn't already being made alive just being in his presence.

His lips scorched me with their warmth. I felt everything I

thought I knew about myself, including my silent suspicion that I was a lesbian, instantly evaporate. This Nigga changed the game right then and there. His tongue slipped across my bottom lip, then into my mouth. My knees buckled. He deftly steadied me in his arms, turning and guiding my body down on to the bed.

I pulled up on his shirt, and he broke the kiss, sitting up to take it off. My mouth wagged open as I read the colorful tattoos of cartoons etched across his chest. Then I pulled his kisses back to me.

Fuck breakfast. Fuck me. I plead silently.

I didn't have to say anything. This Nigga knew what to do. I was in such a trance-like state that I would have suspected I had been drugged, except I hadn't eaten or drunk anything all morning. This hypnotic haze I was in was all from This Nigga and his overwhelming sexual energy. It hung in the air like the scent of his Tommy Hilfiger cologne. I knew I was locked in, but what blew me away was that he seemed locked in too. He groaned intimately in my ear, and I was barely able to make out his strained words.

"I want to make love to you," he whispered.

There was no question to my consent. Any concerns about our age difference resided in a realm of logic that I had abandoned the moment I followed This Nigga down the stairway into the basement.

"Please," was all I could answer. Even that had to be dragged from my vocal cords, which had wilted under the heat of all his passion.

He unbuttoned my shirt and kissed me along my cleavage. These slow, methodical, indulgent kisses drove me wild. They made me feel like he fully appreciated how much there was of me for him to enjoy. It made me want to serve him more and more of me. So when his kisses inched their way lower, there were no thoughts of protesting or pausing the flow. I wanted it all. Whatever This Nigga had to give me, I was ripe for taking. So, I clawed at my pants buckle, unbuttoning and unzipping them as my way of saying "Take what you want from me."

He finished the work of my pants for me. Seconds after that, my whole soul clenched as he went down on me. It was my first time receiving oral sex. This Nigga was a gull grown man. He knew what, where, and how to do it all, and he was doing it all to me. His tongue slipped up and down my labia, dipping deep into me on the down stroke. I stared incredulously at the dome of his bald head. It was nestled comfortably between my legs as if it belonged there. I couldn't fathom how this could possibly be happening to me. It was too good.

Nothing could have prepared me for the experience of my first real orgasm. Up to that point, I thought that I was having orgasms during masturbation because it felt good. I was wrong. Nothing I had ever done to myself, or with anyone else, prepared me for what was about to happen in my body.

First, there was a deep tightening inside of me. Something I'd never felt before was building. The sensation was so shocking that I thought something was wrong with me. Was I dying?

Who cares. Ready heaven...or hell. I'm coming!

Even though I was afraid of what was on the other side of the feeling that was building so quickly within me, I dared not stop him, especially since every brush of his tongue was starting to feel impossibly better than the one before. Then came the tingles. But these weren't the same tingles from the night the house flooded, or even prom night tingles. Those dissipated after a few breaths. This aggressive prickling just intensified with every breath I took. Soon I was gasping uncontrollably. Finally, every muscle in my body contracted for two seconds, then burst into a meteor shower of scintillating pleasure that blinded me for countless minutes. My vision just became a kaleidoscope of colors swirling on the ceiling above us. I howled a sound that could have easily been mistaken for despair or anguish as wave after wave of this orgasm overtook me. My body contorted in spasms as it struggled to find the capacity to handle it all.

I was sure This Nigga had permanently disabled me. The intensity of my climax had peaked, but it was taking its time coming down to a level where I could function. My vision returned first. I realized that my eyes were both leaking tears of pleasure as the tremors continued all over my body. This Nigga sat up in the bed and stared down at me briefly with a look of admiration on his face before laying down beside me. He gathered me up in his arms, pressing me into his chest, which was still blistering to the touch, and soothed me through the last of my quivers. I sank into a deep sleep immediately. I didn't even feel him get out of the bed to go make the breakfast he had promised me.

When I awoke, it was dark in his room. I wasn't sure how much time had passed, but I could smell the scents of breakfast wafting down from upstairs. Soon his body filled the doorway of his bedroom.

"Welcome back," he said with a hint of tease in his voice.

It was far too late to be demure, but I suddenly felt shy. I wasn't sure if all the pieces of me had come back from that orgasm. I felt different.

"How long was I asleep?" I asked.

"Long enough for me to finish breakfast. Now come. Let me feed you," This Nigga crooned.

I wasn't hungry. His tongue had satisfied my appetite. I still took some obligatory bites of the breakfast. I couldn't even taste it. Had This Nigga just ruined all of my senses? It seemed so. He quickly finished his plate, and then also ate what was left on mine when I just couldn't take another bite.

I meandered around the living room while he cleaned up. I hadn't even noticed that I was still naked from the waist down. I'd always been self-conscious of my weight, but I felt perfectly comfortable around him in just my button down shirt.

There was a brown cabinet along the wall displaying a collection of photographs behind glass panels. These included pictures of five young girls of various ages.

"Are these your nieces?" I called over to him in the kitchen.

He poked his head around the corner to see what I was looking at.

"Uhhhh, no," he answered with a pause. "Those are my daughters."

"You...have five daughters?" I swallowed a tiny lump in my throat.

"Yes," he said. "They live on the West Coast with their moms." I stared a little harder at the array of photos. Their skin tones were a variety of shades, but I could see glimpses of him in all of their faces. They all had his eyes and freckles. The youngest looked about nine years old. The oldest was surely a teenager already. I couldn't help thinking I was probably only a few years older than she was. Five daughters? Moms? How many moms?

I decided not to ask any questions I didn't really want the answers to.

When the kitchen was clean, he asked me if I was ready to go. I wasn't.

"Do you want me to go? Are you done with me?" I asked suggestively.

"Never, Beautiful," he responded. I found myself hoping he meant it, but I shook the thought from my head.

I walked over to him, finding an sensual source of confidence inside. When I reached him, I looked up and our eyes locked into each other the same way that had on flood night. Only this time, a different puddle was pooling at my feet. I knew that my face showed a longing for more of him. He gave me the lightest brush of a kiss on the lips. It still hit me like a nuclear shock wave. Then he turned and led me by the hand back downstairs to his room.

This Nigga definitely had more to give. Even though he had dimmed the lights, I could still see that his dick was massive. My eyes struggled to take it all in. It was larger than any I had ever seen in pornography, much less in real life. I was fascinated by its size, and rendered speechless as it hung there, erect in the shadows, like a question in the air. He reached in a small bucket next to his bed and pulled out the answer, a gold Magnum condom.

I climbed onto his bed and laid back, watching him pull the rim of the condom to stretch it over his monster of a cock. Once it was on, he pressed play on a CD changer above my head. A recognizable, breezy jazz tune filled the room. It was "Linus and Lucy" from The Charlie Brown Christmas Movie. I ignored the unusual song selection and chose to put my full attention on preparing to receive him inside of me. I wondered how This Nigga would ever fit.

He eased up on me, resting between my thighs. He kissed me with an emotional intimacy that I fantasized was love. I wanted to make the experience feel more complete when he finally joined me inside. I could feel his penis throbbing against the outside of my pussy, but he acted like he wasn't in any rush at all. I couldn't fathom his self-control. I knew it had come from experience—decades of experience that had made five babies. I blocked the thought of his children from my mind and opened my legs wider, signaling that I was ready to receive him. Just as the piano riffs of Linus and Lucy were changing their key and tempo for the song's breakdown, he began his slow and careful insertion.

I was no virgin, but I still felt some pain in the stretch of his first stroke. I moaned through it, and he responded with another deep kiss while continuing to slip into me, inch by inch. Whenever I thought he was all the way in, he'd go in a little deeper while his tongue circled around mine, creating a perfect distraction from the pain. Finally, I felt the moment when he was as deep inside of me as my young body was capable of receiving. He stayed there for a moment while I marveled at how close we were to each other, inside and out. I never wanted the feeling to end. He ended the stroke with just as much tenderness as it began. I immediately missed the fullness, so I gently bucked my hips up towards him, inviting him back to where I felt he belonged, deep inside of me.

Taking my cue, he took my knee in his hand and gently pushed it up and back as he dug into his second stroke. This time it generated an entirely new sensation of pleasure centered right at the top of my vagina. I learned in that stroke why they call it the G-spot. All I could do was gasp.

"God!" I cried out.

I grasped his neck and held on tight, whimpering and moaning as I found the rhythm with him. I was fully open to him. The immense pleasure was still overwhelming me emotionally, but my body found a way to comply with his every move like I was made to be his.

In my limited previous experience, sexual intercourse had barely lasted a minute or two each time. This Nigga fucked me for what seemed like hours. His staying power was incredible. By the time I detected the staccato in his breathing that signaled his impending arrival, we were both drenched in his sweat which had poured down onto me from his face and upper body. He took both of my legs and wrapped them around his waist, reared back and offered a final stroke before releasing his load into the condom inside of me with a satisfying moan. For the briefest moment, he lost composure and dropped his full weight down on top of me. He sprang right back up and rolled over off of me onto his back as we both struggled to relocate our breath and the ground together.

My mind was blown by the entire experience. I didn't say

anything at all because I couldn't conceive of the words to process it. I had always felt mature beyond my years. But for the first time, I tangibly felt the difference between the adult he was and the child I had been. This was grown up shit. And there I was, lain with him, being schooled at something I had been pretending to know for years. Soon the silence became uncomfortable as my heart rate normalized. I wanted him to be the first to speak, so I could follow his lead and avoid making a fool of myself.

"Was that your first time?" he asked. I thought it an odd question, considering we were beyond the point where it might have mattered.

"For most of it. I was no virgin, but you definitely popped some cherries," I spoke truthfully.

He pulled me close, and I spooned into him and his exhilarating warmth. We snuggled there for a moment before it occurred to me to ask what time it was.

"It's just almost 9:30."

"9:30 PM?" I exclaimed, sitting up with a jerk. I had told my mother I was leaving to go to breakfast over 12 hours before. It was a school night, and I had a 10:00 PM curfew. I worried about explaining to my mother how a morning meal turned into an all day and night outing.

"I have to get home. My mom will kill me if I miss my

curfew," I said.

"Agreed," Then he added, "She'll also kill me if she finds out about this. You're still jailbait."

I had been curious whether or not he remained aware that I was under 18 during our very adult time together. The thought that what we were doing was wrong, potentially even illegal, was frightening, but I was willing to risk it.

"I won't let her find out," I promised.

He reached up and pulled me back down and planted a final and profound kiss on my lips. I'll never forget the next words This Nigga spoke just before we got up to leave.

"I've loved you since the night of the flood. Since the moment I laid eyes on your photograph in Audrey's room, I knew I had to make you mine, " he said.

I didn't respond; I couldn't. This Nigga's sex had already changed me. His love would change my life.

From that date forward, I would frequently sneak out of school to meet up with This Nigga so we could fuck. When This Nigga's parents returned to town, he showed me how to sneak in through the basement's rear exit. He'd leave me standing at the door outside, go open it from the inside, and then quickly shuffle me into his bedroom. He'd put on music, always the Peanuts Soundtrack, to muffle the sounds of my inevitable moans. Then, he would lay it on me.

If we couldn't go to his house, we would go on dates to movies, dinner, or shopping. He worked the night shift at a 24-hour convenience store. His meager hourly wage didn't allow him to pay for most of our dates. But I felt flush with cash from various small scholarship awards. I was happy to make his treats my treat.

When we weren't together, he would call me from work at night. We would talk on the phone for hours, with him only putting me on hold to help customers. Many nights I just fell asleep on the phone with him, grateful for any closeness if I couldn't have physical contact. He ended every conversation with "I love you." Before long, I was saying it back. By the time the school year ended, I believed it.

I skipped school on the morning of my high school graduation to spend the morning with This Nigga. He was coming to my graduation and offered to be my ride. I took everything I needed to get ready. My hair was already done up in intricate curls that died a beautiful death when This Nigga fucked me up against the wall in his bathroom shower. It was our first time having sex outside of his bed. He put me in a different position, taking me from behind. The stroke was so deep I almost couldn't handle it. I was happy to walk with a slight limp and fucked up hair as I ad-libbed my Class President speech, then crossed the stage to receive my high school diploma. Above and out of the sight of my parents below, This Nigga looked on from the balcony, knowing he was responsible for my shaken state. He gave me a proud wave after my name was called, then stood to leave. I had asked him to vacate the ceremony early to avoid the risk of running into my mother.

The thought of This Nigga had me googly-eyed and wild like a Gremlin who ate food after midnight. I felt happy and safe with him. My final weeks at Audrey's house were increasingly bleak. It seemed like the house was falling apart around us, but no one was doing anything about it. I spent as little time there as possible. I had a full-time summer internship at the local telephone company. I had the freedom and the money to stay out and about in between clandestine meetups to date and fuck This Nigga. However, the stretches of hours or days between dates with him left a lot to be desired as we got deeper into the summer. It made me worry about the future, when I left for college.

As the days grew closer to my departure, This Nigga only grew more affectionate and loving towards me. In turn, I showered him with gifts that I paid for with my internship and scholarship money. I also served him all the pussy he could sneak me into his parent's basement to get.

In July, a few weeks before I was scheduled to leave, I took him out for ice cream to celebrate. It had been three months since prom night. We shared his favorite dessert, a banana split.

"With extra cherries on top," he said when he ordered it. He offered with a wink and a smile that made me melt.

After we'd shared our ice cream, This Nigga made an impressive showing of tying a cherry stem into a knot with his tongue. He showed the twisted red twig between his teeth and then gestured for me to hold out my hand. I raised my hand palm up to receive the stem, but instead, he reached out and dropped a silver Claddagh ring into it.

"Marry me," he said, still gripping the cherry stem in his teeth. It wasn't a question. It was a command. It made my 17-year-old heart throb.

I stared at the ring for a moment. It looked like a cheap bauble, but the significance of those two hands meeting at the center to hold up a noble heart was enough for me to believe in it and in him.

"Ok," I answered. Then I wiggled my ring finger in his face until he placed the ring on it.

It was several sizes too big. For a moment I wondered if This Nigga had really picked this ring out for me, and bought it with his own money? Or, had he found it on the street? Or was it a re-gift from one of his baby mamas? That moment didn't last long. What did it matter? It was a ring, for me, backed by a marriage proposal, from a man I loved—a man who loved me.

This was better than my fairytale prom. This was an invitation to a fairytale life where the sexiest, most gorgeous man imaginable chose me out of all the woman in the world.

It didn't matter that the ring was too big. I couldn't wear it anyway. Even though my mother wasn't paying me much attention, I couldn't take a chance of her seeing me wearing an Irish engagement ring. It would raise questions that would force me to create lies I didn't want to tell. So, I put the ring in a box with a lock on it, and kept my engagement to myself.

I had no idea when or how we would get married. One thing I was adamant about was attending college. That fall, I was attending Spelman, one of the best colleges in the country on a full ride scholarship. There was no way I would turn down that opportunity to immediately start my life as This Nigga's wife.

He didn't seem rushed anyway. He said it was a good thing I was going away to school because it gave him some time and space to get his life together and get out of his mother's basement. He also said it gave me some time to come of age. He frequently reminded me that I was still jailbait, and that my mother was a potential threat to our happiness. He was right about that. So, our plan was to get married after my freshman year in college. He would go to computer school in the meantime, and then move to Atlanta to work in IT while I finished college. It all sounded perfect to me.

This Nigga wanted to stop using condoms, so I went on the Pill. Given the size of his penis, I hardly blamed him for hating the condoms. His cock looked like it was suffocating when it was crammed into one. Besides, I preferred the way he felt inside of me without a condom. Something about his skin directly against mine inside of me felt different.

The first time we had sex without a condom, I still asked This Nigga to pull out as an added precaution. His five daughters lulled in the back of my mind. I wasn't about to give him a sixth child. He obliged. He pulled out in time to spray his searing seed onto my belly, then wiped it away with a towel. But after my second month on the Pill, I started allowing him to cum inside me. I loved carrying his warmth around inside of me for a while longer after we made love.

On the eve of my departure for college, This Nigga fucked me so good that I actually thought about not going to college. He took his time and enjoyed himself, savoring me slowly with his mouth. I had worked up the capacity to handle multiple orgasms. I lost count of mine after three. Then he fucked me to an explosive climax. He let loose a savage moan as he unloaded himself inside of me. Afterward, This Nigga hugged me so tightly that I couldn't imagine boarding a plane and flying 1000 miles away from his warmth.

The night came to an end, and we said goodbye until we could be together again in a few months during the holiday break. I was well past my 10:00 PM curfew that night. I figured it didn't matter since I was leaving home for good the next day. Still, I didn't want to risk oversleeping and missing my flight at 6:40 am the next morning. This Nigga dropped me off at the house shortly after midnight.

I was surprised and relieved that my mother wasn't home yet. I figured she was out with her disgusting new boyfriend. As I tiptoed into that house for the last time, I was relieved by her absence. It meant I wouldn't have to answer questions. I climbed the steps to the attic, passing my luggage in the short hallway leading to my room. I had been packed for over a week, which was very unusual for me. I could not have been more ready to leave, even though I was torn about leaving This Nigga behind.

I couldn't sleep. It was after 3:00 AM, and my mother still wasn't home. The light of my TV dimly lit my bedroom in a series of blue shadows and grey lights. I was just starting to nod off when I noticed a strange object fly across the room with a whoosh. I jumped in my bed and reached up to turn on the light. There, flying around in my room, was a gigantic black bat.

I let out a blood-curdling scream and bolted for the bedroom door, dragging my sheet behind me to help cover my naked body, like I had done when my mother's boyfriend broke into our house when I was little. My commotion raised Audrey from her bed and she emerged from her room in a stoned stumble, meeting me on the second level at the bottom of the stairs.

"What's going on?" she asked.

Before I could even gather my breath to answer, the black flash of the bat whizzed by both of our heads, flapping its wings. Audrey and I both ducked down in unison. Out of nowhere, Smokey, the same black cat that had ushered This Nigga into my life by clawing through Audrey's waterbed and causing that epic flood, launched himself into the air with an athletic leap. Smokey snatched the bat from the hallway sky with one skillful paw swipe. Seconds later, Smokey consumed the downed bat. Audrey silently observed the same scene at my side.

"Good Boy," she said to Smokey. She looked at me with an expression that was a mixture of amusement and apathy.

"Good luck at Spelman," she said to me with a toothless grin.

Even though I had seen the bat's demise with my own eyes, nothing could convince me that it was safe to return to that bedroom in the attic. I inched up the stairs to grab my two packed suitcases from the hallway and then stowed away in my mother's room. Her room was empty, as she still wasn't home from where ever she had gone and whatever she was doing.

I counted the minutes, getting worried as they ticked by with no sign of my mother. I wanted to be at the airport by 5:30 AM to check my bags, which meant we needed to leave by 5:00 AM. At 3:45 AM my panic became a plan. I needed help getting to the airport if my mom didn't show. I thought about calling a cab. Instead, I called This Nigga, who answered the phone with a groggy mumble.

"Sorry to wake you but I might need a huge favor. My mom hasn't come home. She is supposed to take me to the airport this morning. If she isn't home in the next 30 minutes, then I need another way to get there. Can you come to get me?" I asked.

"Yes, I will. But I'm sure she'll show up. Every mom wants to see her kid off to college," he replied.

"Not every mom," I said with a voice full of doubt, "I'll call you back if she's still not here in 30 minutes. Get ready to come just in case."

45 minutes later, This Nigga pulled up to the house. We both said nothing as he loaded my bags into the car. I took my seat in the front of his mother's blue Thunderbird and stared at Audrey's house with a frown as he drove me away from it.

Bye Mom.

###

This Nigga-Part 2

This Nigga hugged me goodbye at the airport the morning I left for college. My mother had not shown up to see me off at the airport, so I was grateful for his support.

"Thank you for being here for me," I said, with tiny tears collecting in the corner of my eyes.

"I'm going to be your husband. It's my job to take care of you," he said.

I pressed a small kiss to his lips, took one last look into his green speckled eyes, and then walked away towards the terminal, rolling my life in two large suitcases behind me.

When I was buckled into my seat on the plane, the emotions of my mother's abandonment started to catch up with me. What kind of mother would do this? Not show up. Not say goodbye. The only help I had asked of her for college was a ride to the airport, and she didn't do it. It felt intentional, like an attempt to sabotage my progress. But nothing could have stopped me at that point. I was done being my mother's child; now I was just her daughter.

As the plane took off and ascended to its cruising altitude, I decided to take a forward view. Instead of simmering in anger towards my mother, I focused on This Nigga and his love. I told myself that it was all I needed. I couldn't wait to see the look on my mom's face when I told her we were getting married. I liked This Nigga's plan to wait until after I turned 18 to tell her. I knew it was to serve him, but I felt it was also in my best interest to keep it a secret.

I drifted off and slept the entire flight. After I landed and claimed my bags, I took a taxi from the airport to Spelman's campus. Atlanta sweltered in a thick, humid heat that proved why the city was known as 'Hot-lanta.' The cab driver sat my two large suitcases right on the dusty road of the campus oval in front of my dorm, then drove away. I was on my own moving in. All around me, brand new Spelmanites were being helped by what seemed like generations of proud family members.

Naturally, my dorm was on the third floor, no elevator. It took me two trips to get my bags up the stairs. Only as I was mounting the last segment of the stairs with my second bag did a man wearing a 'Spelman Dad' t-shirt stop to help me as he was coming down the stairs. I wheezily thanked him as if he'd saved my life, since I did feel like I was dying from the exertion and heat.

I knew I had two roommates named Samantha and Darlene. They were both from California. Their addresses had been typed onto the dorm assignment card I had received in the mail only two weeks before leaving. My name was just written in pen across the top of the card. I sent them both postcards with my contact information, but I didn't hear back from either of them as I had hoped. I figured that the three of us would have the entire year to get to know each other at Spelman.

I dragged my bags down through the halls of the third floor until I reached my door. I swung it open and was surprised to find it already filled with people. Both of my roommates had already arrived, accompanied by their families.

The group stopped its conversation and looked at me in shock when I entered the room. I looked around and immediately came to understand why everyone seemed so surprised to see me. I also realized why my name had been hand-written on the dorm assignment card. The room was a double, not a triple. But, in the center of the room that was already set up with two beds, two dressers, two desks, and two closets, the college had added an additional set of furniture—my furniture. I was crashing this room.

Samantha was the first of my roommates to greet me. She was skinny and short, with long box braids raining down her back. With a bright smile, Samantha introduced me to her mother, her grandmother, and her high school best friend who had all joined her for college move-in day. I envied the amount of support she had with her. My other roommate, Darlene was a taller girl, with light-brown skin that revealed her mixed race. Her hair framed her face in sweaty curls. She was only there with her mother, a small, older white woman who stood out amidst all the brown faces in the crowded dorm room.

I introduced myself to Samantha and Darlene with a handshake and an apology.

"I'm KishaLynn. Sorry, I guess they just kinda stuck me in here with you guys," I said. I'm sure my own face showed how helpless I felt in this situation.

Darlene's mother stepped forward.

"It's ok. We'll make do with it," she offered optimistically. "Let's rearrange this furniture. The room clearly isn't going to work like this."

We all went to work pushing and moving furniture around in the stifling 100+ degree room until we found a configuration that worked down to the last inch of space available. Our three beds were lined up next to each other from the door to the window on the wall, with only two feet of space between them. We could only get two of the dressers to fit around the remaining perimeter of the room and still have access to our three desks. I crammed my dresser into one of the closets—a tiny walk-in. It was such a tight fit that I was sure the piece of furniture would live there forever. Samantha and Darlene, who had already forged a bond over the summer, agreed to share the second closet.

It wasn't perfect, but it was done. My roommates departed to go eat with their families, leaving me alone and in envy. It stung a bit that none of them invited me to join, but I also understood. They didn't owe me anything. My existence in the space was inconvenience enough.

I found a payphone in the hallway and dialed home. There was no answer. Next, I called This Nigga to tell him I had arrived safely.

"Ok, Beautiful. Enjoy yourself out there. I love you," he said, soothing my heart.

I realized I didn't want to be there, so far away from him and so alone. I didn't want the call to end.

"I've gotta run to work. Until soon, Beautiful."

We hung up, and I started crying in the pay phone booth.

Where the fuck is my mother?

After many attempts to call, I finally connected with my mother on my third day at college. Audrey put her on the phone.

"Hello?" she said. She sounded groggy as if she'd just woken up, but it was well after 3:00 PM.

"Mom, I only asked you for one thing to help with college. All I needed was a ride to the airport. Where were you?"

"Sorry," she said, sounding anything but. "I overslept."

"Why haven't I been able to reach you for three days?"

"I've been busy. The world doesn't revolve around you, you know!" she responded.

That was all she had to say. It was enough to tell me what I needed to know. She didn't care.

"I've gotta go mom. Goodbye," I said, hanging up.

College was nothing like I had fantasized it would be. I began to question my choice of institution immediately. Spelman was supposed to be such a big deal. However, on the campus, surrounded by other young black women, I ironically felt out of place from the start. The University of Illinois at Chicago was initially my first choice school. But when the Spelman College acceptance letter arrived, coupled with an separate offer of a full scholarship from my benefactor, I was personally dazzled into going to Spelman for its prestige. I had planned to go to a large, co-ed, state university in a major city that was close to home. Instead, I was at a small, historically black college, liberal arts college for women in the south, hundreds of miles away from any family. It couldn't be more different than what I had hoped for.

I wanted to complain to This Nigga about it more, but our calls were far and few between. He told me he wasn't able to continue talking on the phone while he worked. That limited his availability to hours when I was usually in class or at dinner. Still, I would skip both every few days just to hear his voice. I tried to compel him to learn how to email and chat on the Internet since that was still my preferred form of communication.

"That's why I'm gonna go to computer school, Beautiful. To learn that stuff," This Nigga said one day when I bugged him about it.

"You don't need computer school to send an email. I've been doing it since I was 15!" I argued back.

Then I wrote him a step-by-step instruction manual on how to set up and use a free email account, giving him access to my Internet service provider login. He followed the steps and sent me one email, but that didn't result in any more regular written communications between us.

I picked up a new friend in my dorm, a light-skinned Texan named Simone. She was sweet as could be when I met her, washing her hair in the dorm laundry room. Spelman had banned hair washing in the showers, so we had to go down to the basement to shampoo. It was one of the things I thought was ridiculous about the college, along with prohibiting the disposal of sanitary napkins in the bathroom trash. I knew I shared something in common with Simone when we were both washing our hair instead of attending the first co-ed party of the year, celebrating the end of freshman orientation. Spelman had finally opened its gates to let the Morehouse Men loose on us tender freshman Spelman Women. Simone and I had both opted out. We laughed about our lameness and our shared commitment to good hair. I knew we would be instant friends.

Simone had a boyfriend who was away at a different college.

We bonded over the challenges of maintaining long-distance relationships. Her boyfriend regularly sent her flowers and gifts, which made me feel envious. I shared with her that I was engaged to This Nigga back at home. She was happy to dream out loud with me about my wedding. We even went shopping for bridal magazines. I became obsessed with reading them in my large chunks of free time, picking colors and flagging potential dresses.

One person who didn't have much to say about a wedding, or marriage, or virtually anything at all was This Nigga. I finally had my own phone line in my room, but he hardly ever called. My anxiety levels always rose when a few days passed without hearing from him. When I did reach him, he would assure me that he was merely working hard trying to save money for computer school.

"So that we can stick to the plan, right?" I offered, needing him to throw me a bone.

"Yeah. That's right, Beautiful. The plan to move to Atlanta and make you my wife."

That would put me back over the moon, for a few days anyway.

When the summer finally began to cool into fall, I detected even more distance between us. I was hurt when This Nigga missed my 18th birthday on September 6. It was a Sunday. I spent the entire day in my room, waiting for his call. I finally heard back from him four days later. He apologized profusely for not calling, so I forgave him. No one else had cared about my birthday either. There was no point in taking it out on him.

Besides, I didn't want to waste the time I had talking to him on an argument. I needed to bring us together, not push him away. We were only talking once a week, and he was becoming less and less engaged in our conversations. One night I called This Nigga out on it.

"You sure are short of words these days. What's going on?" I asked.

"Nothing's going on, Beautiful. I'm just tired all the time," he answered.

"Are you sure that's it? I mean, I feel like you were tired before, when I was home, but you always made time for me. For us," I said.

"I know, Beautiful. I'm sorry. I guess I just miss you. I wish you could come home," he said.

"That's possible. That's definitely possible. I'll just fly home to see you. Would you be able to help me out with the costs of a flight and room?" I asked.

"Sure. Just let me know how much," This Nigga agreed.

It was important to me that he contributed money to the trip. When had I last seen him, I was flush with cash and generous with it. However, I was now running low on scholarship funds after spending so much of it on him that summer. Only three of my scholarships were renewable. So once I blew through the thousands of dollars in one-time scholarships I'd received that summer, my income was limited to $1500 per semester from the renewable scholarships. It was a flat-out miracle that the full-ride scholarship I had received paid for 100% of my tuition, room, board, and books. All I really needed money for was personal care items, and air travel to and from home. But my habit for wasting money on dining out had taken a toll on my savings that semester. I was starting to be really mindful of my funds.

On the other hand, I felt that a special visit home to see This Nigga was just what we both needed—quality time to conserve our love. Plus, it was an opportunity for me to see what it was like to spend the night and wake up next to him in the morning. So I used a chunk of my remaining scholarship savings to purchase a flight for a one-night visit in October.

Something felt off from the moment I was in This Nigga's arms again at the airport. Barely two months had passed, yet he looked like he had aged a couple of years. I pouted a little when he didn't kiss me. His kiss was a touch that I had been yearning for every moment since I had left for college. He just hugged me quickly before loading my carry-on bag into his mom's rusty but trusty Thunderbird. Then, we were off.

We'd never been to a hotel together before. In my mind, I had fantasized it as a romantic secret rendezvous. I was a little sad that we weren't able to return to the nostalgic cave of This Nigga's bedroom and have my moans join the chorus of 'Linus and Lucy' in the air again.

When we settled into the hotel room, it was almost 4:00 PM. I looked at him expectantly for a grand gesture. What I got was a yawn as he emptied his pockets on the drawer, then stretched out across the bed. I joined him there, snuggling myself up under his arm looking for a space that I always fit perfectly into. His body temperature wasn't quite as warm as I remembered it, but he was still comfortable to lie beside.

"You tired?" I asked.

"Yeah. Worked a double shift so I could take tonight off with you. I haven't slept in about two days," he replied.

"Oh. OK. Well, I'm fine if you need a nap," I offered.

He sat up and leaned over to kiss me. Relief rushed through me as I mistook the gesture to mean he was choosing me instead of sleep. I leaned back into the kiss, expecting more.

"Thanks, Beautiful. I'll just have a short nap."

My relief vanished as quick as it had come.

He fell asleep, and I watched TV, wondering why things didn't feel quite right.

This Nigga slept for over six hours. By the time he even stirred, it was after 10:00 PM. I was hungry and more than a little annoyed. He opened one eye to peek out at me from his slumber.

"Hey, Beautiful," he said. I looked at down at him.

"Hey. Welcome back." I said. I remembered how he had used the same words after he ate me out to completion for the first time on the morning after prom night and I'd passed out cold for hours.

"I'm starving. Let's go eat," he said.

This Nigga wanted to go to his favorite pizza restaurant in Copley Place. But, I was paranoid about bumping into my mother, or anyone I knew, since I wasn't supposed to be home from school for a few more weeks. Even though I was already 18, it felt too risky. I also wanted to stay close to the room, in hopes of getting close with him in what was left of the evening. So we agreed to walk over to a burger place across the street from the hotel instead.

"As long as it has a bar, it'll work for me," he said.

We were seated in a back booth at the restaurant. This Nigga immediately ordered a beer. I ordered a soda. We studied menus for a moment and placed our order. Now we finally had no choice but to look at each other face-to-face. He looked so much older to me. I wondered if I looked older to him. Did he feel relieved that I was 18 now? I struggled to hide my disappointment about how long he had slept at the hotel, and how little attention he had paid me since I arrived. I knew I was acting like a child. He was rested now. Besides, I wouldn't be there if he hadn't asked me to come. He wanted me there.

But our conversation over dinner was lackluster.

“How’s work?” I asked.

“It’s work,” He downed his first beer and ordered another one.

“Did you decide on a computer school program yet?”

“No. I’ve been too busy working and saving money.”

That gave me hope, so I decided not to press my luck with more questions. I prattled on about school for a moment, sharing how I wasn’t sure I’d made the right choice in colleges. I was thinking about transferring. He was barely listening to me.

"How would you feel about not living in Atlanta?" I asked. The question seemed to throw him out of a reverie he was experiencing chewing his burger and fries and chasing it down with gulps of beer.

“Huh? Oh. I’ll go wherever you are, Beautiful,” he responded.

The answer wasn’t entirely satisfying for me, but I was holding fast to best of the moment. Meanwhile, This Nigga ordered a third round of beer.

He asked for the check when the waitress dropped his third beer, then proceeded to chug it down. I hadn’t known him to drink so much before I left. The more I thought about it though,

I did recall that he liked to have a beer on our dates.

He reached in his pocket and pulled out his wallet. He counted out a few bills and handed them to me. It was $90.

"That's half of the money I owe you for the trip. I'll get the rest to you in a couple of weeks when I get paid again," he said. Then, This Nigga put his wallet away.

I looked down at the check for a moment before reaching across and picking it up from the table. I guessed dinner would be on me. Then I put two of the $20 bills he'd just given me into the bill folder and stood up to leave.

When we got back to the room, he seemed to have more energy. I wasn't sure if it was the rest, the food, or the beer but for a moment it seemed like This Nigga was back to his usual charming self. He pulled me close to him, and we kissed. His kisses were rushed and a bit messy considering that for once, we didn't have to stare at the clock. We had all of what was left of that night, plus the following morning before I had to leave him again in the afternoon the next day.

He began to claw at my clothes, so I helped him out a bit by taking my own clothes off. As I stripped down, I hoped that he could smell the special perfume I had borrowed from Simone. He pressed his body against mine, and I tumbled clumsily back on the bed. I recovered, sitting up to work at his belt buckle. He stepped back and removed his pants.

The first thing I noticed was that his penis not hard. That had never happened. His cock was always stiff and ready, stretching towards me when I laid eyes on it. This time, his penis looked like it needed another six-hour nap. I looked up at him with a question in my eyes.

He ignored it with a sigh and took off his sweatshirt. Then he pushed me back and dropped to his knees to give me oral sex. It was far less magical than before, in part because I couldn't get the thought of his flaccid penis out of my head. But also, he wasn't doing it the way he had before I left. Instead of taking his time and making me feel savored, his mouth moved sloppily around my loins as if he was lost, or bored. I tried to orgasm. I wasn't used to having a choice in the matter. After a while, I stopped him.

"Sorry," I said. "I guess I'm the one who's tired now."

He smiled at me a bit. "It's ok, Beautiful." Then he stood up. His penis was erect now, and I knew he was finally ready to fuck me.

I had remained on the birth control pill at college, so I didn't bring condoms. This time, of all times, I didn't want anything between us as we made love. I just knew this was the moment when everything would fall back into place. Whenever he was deep inside of me, I felt my most complete. I laid back and waited for him to make me whole again.

He came inside of me after only a few strokes. Then, he

rolled over on his side and fell asleep. I laid there in the dark, crushed. I wondered what had changed.

Does he not love me anymore? Is it because I'm 18 now? Maybe it was hotter when it was wrong.

I stared at his body, covered in a sheet, rising and falling with each breath, wondering what happened.

Could it be that This Nigga is no longer attracted to me?

I was so used to feeling like the most beautiful woman in the world when around him. Now I didn't even feel like I was his woman. I wondered if there was someone else.

He had an electronic Rolodex. I had seen him set it on the hotel dresser with his wallet earlier after emptying his pockets. I climbed out of bed and walked over to it. I hesitated for a minute before picking it up. I felt like he deserved my trust if I was going to marry him. On the other hand, he was definitely being weird. I had to know if there was another woman involved. So I pressed the power button and scrolled quickly through the contacts.

There weren't many. My name was in it, spelled incorrectly. I ignored that. Everyone spelled my name wrong.

There were some male names I didn't recognize. It never occurred to me that he might have friends outside of Audrey's son. Then at the bottom of the contacts was a list of female names. Naturally, I didn't recognize any of them. This Nigga hadn't introduced me to any friends. It's not like he wanted to show off his 17-year-old girlfriend to anyone. But these names bothered me tremendously. Who were these women? Was he seeing them? Were they his daughter's names? His baby mamas?

There was no way to tell without revealing that I had snooped. I closed the Rolodex and climbed back into bed with him. He didn't budge. The sheets were cold. I had missed his warmth so much. But as I laid there beside him, I realized I might as well have been lying in my dorm room bed. I usually cried in bed alone at school because I missed him so much. I cried in bed that night beside him because he obviously didn't feel the same. Nothing felt the same anymore. I didn't know what it meant. Or maybe I didn't want to admit that I did know.

Morning came slowly. This Nigga slept past 10:00 AM. The very second he stirred, I sat up in bed and delivered a frantic series of inquiries.

"What happened?!? Is it me? You not attracted to me anymore? Is there someone else?" I asked.

"Whoa, whoa, whoa," he said, rubbing his eyes. "First of all, good morning."

"Good morning," I replied, tartly. "I sure am glad I flew all the way out here to watch you sleep."

He sighed and threw his head back in the pillow.

"I'm tired! I explained to you that I had to work a double just to be here," he said.

"I know that, but I came all this way to see you. I was hoping things would be different. Now I'm leaving again in a few hours, and we haven't spent any time together." I was able to hold back tears, though I felt my chin trembling.

This Nigga pulled me back down onto the bed and wrapped me in his arms.

"Look, I'm sorry it's not going the way you had hoped. I didn't expect to be this tired either. It's just one of those things that happens."

I looked up at his face, resisting the urge to count the freckles there that I loved so much. Instead, I looked into his eyes, searching them for truth that was hidden behind bloodshot whites and pupils that had lost some of their emerald shine. If only he would make love to me like he had the night before I left. I had expected him to pour himself into me during this trip. Instead, I felt him pulling out. We were still for a while. I was sure there was nothing more he could give me sexually; it just wasn't going to happen. I broke from his embrace and started gathering up my things.

"Let's go eat. Check out is at noon, and my flight leaves at 2:00 PM," I said.

There was something in This Nigga's hug goodbye at the airport that told me that we were done. No matter how hard I tried to create a romantic moment between us, it wasn't working.

This Nigga's brief kiss was flavored with the pungent spice of the end.

“Love you, Beautiful,” he said, as I slung my bag over my shoulder.

“I love you too. See you in a few weeks.” My voice carried more hope than my heart.

I looked at him for a moment longer before I turned to head into the airport. I knew it wouldn’t be the last time I’d see him, but it felt like the last time he’d be mine when I looked at him. He was off with a quick wave.

Simone met me at the airport to pick me up.

"How was it?" She asked as we boarded the MARTA train together. I wanted to tell the truth, that it was terrible. I was tempted to lie and say that it was terrific. Instead, I opted for ambiguity.

"It was cool. I am exhausted. I didn’t get much sleep," I answered.

She looked at me with a smile.

"Lucky," she said.

I gave a slight smile back but offered no further details affirming or denying my fortune. I was crushed by the outcomes of the visit. There was no point in disappointing Simone with a recount of his flaccid penis, his sloppy head, his two-minute stroke, and his 16 hours of sleep. So I leaned my head against the window of the subway and pretended to doze off.

After a full night's rest back at school, I formulated my plan. I would break up with This Nigga and see what he said. If he loved me so much and wanted to marry me, then he would fight for me, right? He wouldn't just let me walk away. I had to know. I didn't want to lose him, but breaking up was the only way I knew to test his love for me.

His mother answered the phone when I called. I hated when that happened. As I held the line waiting for her to get This Nigga on the phone, I practiced what I was going to say.

"Hello," I heard his voice speak on the line.

"Hi, it's me. I made it back to campus," I started.

"Oh ok. I'm getting ready for work," he said, sounding rushed.

"Yeah, I am not going to keep you. Just wanted to let you know I made it back." I took a deep breath. "Actually, also, I called to break up with you. Things just didn't feel right while I was there, and I don't think we should be together anymore."

There was a moment of silence in the line, and for a moment I thought he was in shock. I waited, hoping for his heart to change at the thought of losing me.

"Ok. Cool," he said. I was sure I heard This Nigga wrong.

"Cool?" I repeated.

"Yeah. Is that it?" He said.

"Well, yes, I guess it is," I replied.

"All right. Well, I have to get to work. Take care," he said.

I hung up the phone and sat there in silence. This Nigga hadn't made a single attempt to fight for me, or for us. It was just over. I thought I was smart when I devised this test; I didn't expect This Nigga to fail it.

My heart was too broken for tears at that moment. Those would come in ample amounts later. I reached up and pulled our prom photos down from the short section of wall I had next to my bed. I took one last look at the two of us together on that magical night, then packed the images away in a box along with all the other visible evidence of our love. I abstained from contacting him, but lived by my phone hoping for a call signifying This Nigga's changed heart. It never came.

I couldn't resist the urge to contact This Nigga the second I landed in Boston for Thanksgiving Break a few weeks later. I called him from a payphone at the airport. The moment he heard my voice, he told me he couldn't talk and ended the call, making me feel the fool that I was.

How can a man who I thought loved every part of me, in just a few weeks time, want no part of me at all?

I did an excellent job of hiding my torment throughout the week of Thanksgiving at home. I had no one to talk to about the pain I felt, so I wrote letters to This Nigga, apologizing to him. I felt sorry for being stupid enough to test his love by throwing it away. In my letters, I begged him not to let my foolishness be the way our beautiful love story ended.

I wrote letters every night, but I never sent them. I told myself I couldn't risk This Nigga's mother intercepting them. But I knew I just couldn't face the pain of him ignoring my heartfelt words. I dreamed of the day we would read the letters together and laugh about how our love almost got away from us. I tried to believe that this self-inflicted breakup was temporary.

When Thanksgiving break ended with no reconciliation, I returned to college resolving myself to somehow restore our relationship by Christmas. But first, I needed to focus on my final exams. The fall semester had been a difficult start for me academically. I managed to squeak by, using the pressure my procrastination created to power through, rather than letting it undo me. Work had always been an excellent distraction from pain.

At the start of finals week, I visited the Health Center for a physical appointment I had scheduled earlier in the semester. I was hoping to get my birth control prescription refilled.

However, the college policy was to administer examinations, including a Pap smear, before they would prescribe or even refill birth control. I told them I had just had an exam earlier that year when I got the prescription, but they refused to refill my pills without doing their own physical. I gave in and scheduled the appointment for December, weeks before my current prescription was due to run out. I thought about canceling the appointment since I had broken up with This Nigga, but I figured better safe than sorry. I endured the exam and walked out with a prescription for three more months of birth control. I prayed I would need it when I went home.

The day before my flight home to Boston for the Christmas break, I got a call from the student health center.

“We need to see you down here as soon as possible,” a woman’s voice said on the other line.

“Why? I already got my birth control refilled,” I asked.

“We need to discuss some of the lab results from your physical,” she responded.

For a fleeting second, I panicked. Had This Nigga somehow gotten me pregnant? No, it couldn’t be. I had visited him in October. I had gotten my period over the Thanksgiving break and another was due any day.

“I’m leaving for the holiday break tomorrow, and I have a lot to pack. Can I come when we get back to school in January?" I asked. I really didn't want to go; I had a bad feeling about it.

"No. I need you to come down here, today. We close at 4:00 PM. Can you come over right now?"

Something in her voice said she meant business. I couldn't fathom what would be so urgent if it wasn't a baby. Since I was confident I wasn't pregnant, and that was the worst scenario imaginable, I agreed to go in.

"Yeah, I'll be over in 10 minutes," I said.

The student health center, like much of campus, was void of students. The silence was eerie. I had only visited once before, and then it was bustling with activity. This visit it was so empty and quiet I had to call out to get someone's attention.

"Hello? Anyone?" I called out.

"Kisha?" asked a middle-aged black woman who walked out into the lobby to greet me wearing pink floral scrubs and holding a medical record file. I recognized her as the voice on the phone and the same nurse practitioner that was explained to me that she couldn't refill my birth control without an exam.

"Yeah," I said slowly. I didn't bother correcting my name.

"Come on back with me." She said, holding open the same door for me that she had walked through.

When we were closed together in a tiny exam room, she

opened the medical record file and had a quick look at it.

"Thanks for coming over so quickly. We try to process and review all the labs before the break, but it gets busy over here. Anyway, I'm glad I caught you because I have to inform you that one of your test results came back positive. Unfortunately, you have Chlamydia." she said.

The word did not compute in my brain.

Chlamydia. What was that? I was sure it was bad, but it didn't sound like anything terrible that I'd ever heard of, like cancer. Besides, I hadn't even been feeling sick, outside of my heartache. I blinked at the lady, who could instantly see my lack of understanding.

"Chlamydia is a sexually transmitted infection," she added.

Her words roared through my eardrums like a tidal wave on their way to my brain. Once there, they receded just as quickly, tearing my soul at the seams along the way.

"Did you just say I have an STD?" I asked. I couldn't even remember or pronounce the word to say it back to her.

"Well, Chlamydia is sexually transmitted, but it's not a disease. It's an infection. A bacterial infection."

"How can I have...a sexual...disease...infection?" I asked. I could hear distress increasing in my voice as I struggled to understand what was happening.

“Have you had unprotected sex? Without a condom?” She asked flatly, knowing the answer.

"Well, yes with my…" my voice faded off. The nurse didn’t need to know the answer to that too. I barely knew what to call This Nigga myself.

“You’re on the birth control pill, but that doesn’t protect you from sexual diseases and infections like this. Only abstinence can.” The word abstinence hung in the air for a second.

“Am I going to die?” I felt my face go pale.

She sighed out loud.

"No. Thank the good Lord Chlamydia is one we can cure. You got lucky."

Even she cringed at her poor choice of words. In a moment of short-lived compassion, I realized she had probably had much worse conversations in that tiny exam room. The thought passed when I snapped back to my own terrible moment with her.

“What’s the cure?” I asked, already feeling disgusting from head to toe.

“It’s an antibiotic drink I’ll mix for you to take here today in one big dose. In seven days the Chlamydia will be cured.”

“Ok. Can I take it now?”

“Yes, but first I’ll need you to complete some paperwork.”

She opened my file, pulled out a couple of papers, and handed them over to me.

"Please fill this top form out for me." she began.

"This paper is information about Chlamydia and the treatment you are about to receive. You keep that."

"And this," she said, pausing for a moment. "This is important information for you about notifications. Make a list of your sexual partners from the past six months. You will need to contact them all to notify them of your test results. Inform them that they may be infected and encourage them to be tested. I'll be right back with the medicine."

I glanced down at the notifications sheet on top, which provided a suggested script for me to use to notify my sexual partners of my test results. Then below it was a space for me to list their names and numbers for easier reference in reaching out.

I took the pen and wrote This Nigga's name and number on the top line. Then I set the pen down. A tear fell out of my eye and landed onto the table next to it.

This dirty motherfucker. When and how did he get Chlamydia? And how could I be so stupid to allow him to pass it on to me?

In the past, I had been a stickler for safe sex. I had insisted on putting condoms on with my own hands to ensure it was done correctly. I never did that with This Nigga. For the brief period that we used condoms, I liked to watch him put it on. I failed miserably the one and only time I tried to take his massive cock in my hands and force a condom onto it.

Then I had gone on the birth control pill. I threw all cares about safe sex right out the window with the box of condoms. This Nigga and I were in love. I didn't want anything, even latex, separating the two of us during sex—as long as I couldn't get pregnant.

There I sat in the health center, burnt. The fact that the condition was curable was barely a consolation.

The nurse returned holding a silver tray with a box, a paper cup, a pitcher of water, and a tongue depressor on it. She set it down gently, then put on some gloves.

"This is an oral medication. I'll mix it up for you here, then you take it all down, followed by another full cup of water. Then, don't engage in any sexual activity for the next seven days. After a week, the antibiotic in this medication will have cured the infection."

She picked up the box and pulled out a pouch, tearing it open and pouring its contents, a purple powder, into the cup, then covering it with water from the pitcher. Next, she ripped the paper off the tongue depressor and used it to stir the concoction well. Finally, she picked up the cup and handed it to me.

"I believe this is grape flavored. Anyway, drink up." Then she added, "Please remember there is no such thing as safe sex. But if you must, always use a condom."

I choked down the bitter elixir, which indeed had a grape aftertaste. As I swallowed it, I remembered the last time I had STD testing. Just before I graduated, I had made an appointment at the local health center at home because I was experiencing intense burning when I urinated. It had turned out that my vagina was torn, undoubtedly from the girth of This Nigga's penis. I was given a medicated douche to use twice a day for a week until the tear healed. Later in the mail, I had also received notification of negative STD results. I was clean when I left for college. So how did This Nigga get the Chlamydia he had clearly passed on to me in October?

It was obvious that he had cheated on me since I left. I felt like a fool for not taking precautions and making him wear a condom when I snuck home. I trusted him and believed we were getting married. In my supreme immaturity and stupidity, I was blinded by love.

After I finished the drink, the nurse refilled the cup with water and asked me to drink that too. I gulped it down, eager to wash the taste of the 'Chlamydicure' away. I crushed the paper cup in my hand before setting it back on the tray. Then, wiping another tear from the corner of my eye, I looked at the nurse.

"Is that all?" I asked, struggling to hold it together. I didn't want to break down in front of her.

"Yes hon, we're done. Take your paperwork. Don't put off

the notifications. The sooner you take care of it, the better. Enjoy your holiday break."

Once I was alone again, I was sure I would die from the heartbreak. It felt like my heart was imploding in my chest. I needed a shoulder to cry on, but most students had already left. My flight home wasn't until the next morning. I went to Simone's room and was relieved to find her still there. She was closing up her luggage and preparing to catch her flight home that evening. When she opened her door, she was taken aback by my bewildered state. I collapsed into her arms, finally letting loose the fullness of my tears and my pain. In a jumble of barely coherent sentences, I revealed to her the dirty truth about a love I thought was pure and real with This Nigga. Then I slid from her arms down to my knees on her floor and laid there crying until I was retching from my sobs. She reached down to comfort me.

"Don't touch me!!! I am tainted and dirty!" I screamed.

Simone kept her distance but crouched down to my level to look me in the eye.

"You are not dirty or tainted, Darling," she said. "He is. He did this to you. But don't worry. God will take care of you. And Hell will take care of him."

This comforted me immensely. I was able to bring my sobs under control.

"Can I please stay in here until you have to go? I can't bear to be alone just yet," I asked.

"Of course you can. My roommate also leaves tomorrow, so if you need to stay here, I am sure she will be fine with that." I had seen her roommate enter the room in the midst of my breakdown. She had swiftly made an about-face to exit when she observed the crisis unfolding there, adding to my embarrassment.

"I'll just stay until you leave. Thank you," I said.

I remained on the floor, still crying, but quietly now. I must have dozed off because soon Simone was tapping me on my shoulder and telling me her taxi had arrived. She gave me a big hug before we parted ways. She was headed to the airport and a flight home. I was facing the longest, saddest, loneliest night ever in my dorm room. I moved numbly through the motions of packing the last of my bags for the holiday break, then I took a scalding hot shower before falling into bed weary from the emotion of the day.

The next morning I woke up feeling just as wounded on the inside but looking passably functional when I glanced in the mirror. I was done crying, but my eyes carried a shroud of sadness—I had never seen my irises, which were normally hazel in color, look so dark and my skin had never looked so pale. But, I was standing, and that was enough. It was time to go back to Boston. I would be staying with my mom, who had no clue about This Nigga and what he did to me. I had to face This Nigga with the difficult news. At the same time, I had to deal with the reality that my life wasn't going to include his love anymore—ever.

Once again, the moment I was on the ground in Boston, I found a pay phone at the airport and dialed This Nigga's mother's house, taking advantage of the opportunity to discreetly call him without having to pay long distance.

He answered on the third ring. I was relieved that I didn't have to ask his mother to speak to him. I got straight to the point.

"It's me. I need to see you. It's absolutely urgent, and we must talk face to face. When are you available?" I asked.

"Uhhh…" I heard him stalling on the other line.

"Look, meet with me this one time, and I guarantee I'll never ask to see you again." Then, in a moment of wisdom, I added, "I'm not pregnant if that's what you're thinking."

"Oh good!" he said. His insolence made me nauseous.

"I need to go buy some painting supplies for a project here tomorrow. If you want to meet me at Mattapan Station, we can take a walk down to the hardware store together and catch up. Around noon?" He suggested.

"Fine. I'll meet you at Mattapan Station at noon tomorrow. But listen, if you don't show, you'll leave me no choice but to come to you. Please don't make me do that." Then I hung up on This Nigga and made my way towards my mother's house.

It was bitterly cold the next day as I made my way from my mother's place in Roslindale to Mattapan Station on the subway. I got off of the train at Ashmont Station and switched over to the cable car trolley that would take me to Mattapan. Nostalgic memories of past clandestine meet-ups with This Nigga clogged my heart and brain. This was going to be a very different meeting.

The notification form I had received from the nurse in the Student Health Center was folded in my winter coat pocket. This Nigga was the sole name listed on it. As the trolley lumbered along the historic streets of Boston, I mouthed the script, practicing the mortifying words a few times. I tried to imagine what his reaction would be when I broke the news.

I had a plan to walk straight to his house from the trolley if he wasn't there. It was a walk I had done with him plenty of times under far better circumstances. Fortunately, he was standing there when my trolley arrived at three minutes past noon. He was wearing a brown trench coat jacket, but no hat or gloves. That was crazy for a December in Boston, but he had always run warm.

I approached him with a purpose in my stride, walking past him to avoid any type of hug he might offer, regardless of how badly I wanted one. His touch was poison, and my only purpose on this day was to let him know that.

"Come on, let's walk," I said, leading the way even though he had picked the destination.

He caught up and walked silently beside me for a moment. I couldn't even look at him. In part, because I was angry, but also I was still vulnerable to him, his looks, and his charm. I was afraid that if he even tried just a little bit, I would lose myself in the same false hope that had brought me to that very moment. So I focused on my feet, walking at a steady pace.

"How have you been?" He started. I was annoyed by how casual he could be.

"Honestly, I've been much better. Not that I expect you to care. I know you don't." There was bitterness in my voice that felt colder than the wind chill. I hoped he heard it.

"Of course I care," he said with a softness that I almost believed.

Don't get pulled in KishaLynn. Do what you came to do.

"Well, since you care so much," I said, my voice laced with sarcasm, "Then I'll just come right out with it." I stopped walking and stared up at him, making eye contact for the first time since I'd snuck home to see him.

Stick to the script.

"I tested positive for Chlamydia. It's a sexually transmitted infection." I paused only to grit my teeth for a second and thrust the notification paper into his hand before continuing.

"Since you have been my only sexual partner, that means that you are likely infected with Chlamydia as well. You will need to get tested, and treated. Fortunately, Chlamydia is curable. I can't really say the same for what you've done to me." I delivered my statement with poignant clarity. Then I resumed walking.

A few short moments later he fell back into step beside me. He folded the paper and stuck it into a pocket in his trench coat. We were silent for the next block, with several more blocks to walk before we reached the hardware store.

"Aren't you going to say anything?" I said, impatiently breaking the stifling quietness.

"I'll go get checked out," he replied.

I whipped my head around to look at This Nigga.

"Is that all?" I cried out, sounding more desperate than I wanted to.

"Well, yeah. What do you want me to say? Oops?"

Blind rage overcame me, obliterating all hope that This Nigga would do something to make this better for me. I held my composure with remarkable self-control, stomping along the road beside him for another block, calculating my response.

"I thought that might be all you have to say for yourself. I must be the biggest idiot who ever loved you. I'm sure the list is long," I replied.

To that, he merely let out a long sigh.

As we reached the parking lot of the hardware store, I felt tears beginning to break through. I had indeed hit rock bottom with This Nigga; it was covered in the shards of my shattered heart.

You will not cry in front of This Nigga. You are not a child anymore KishaLynn. If you ever were. Be strong.

I walked him to the door of the hardware store. I was struggling to breathe at that point. Frosty air puffed up around me with every exhale. I stopped short as he entered the store. He turned around and looked at me.

"You coming?" He asked.

"No. I've said all I have to say. Besides, I've followed you enough. I'm done." There was a firm finality in my voice that even I believed.

"Ok, well thanks for letting me know about the situation. Again, sorry," he said.

"No one is sorrier than me," I said, glaring at him for the instant I dared to make eye contact.

"Thank you too," I continued, "For finally giving me a reason not to love your sorry ass anymore."

With that I turned and walked away, hurrying my step

unnecessarily. This Nigga wasn't giving chase. When I looked back, he had already vanished into the doors of the store.

Once I was beyond the parking lot of the hardware store, my step began to stagger a bit. I broke down into tears that burned when they met the cold winds whipping against my face. I was walking into the wind now. The sting felt almost cathartic.

Each step made me feel like I was dying a thousand tiny deaths. I knew falling into love with This Nigga carried the risk of pain like this, but nothing prepared me for the reality of it.

As I neared the train station, I reminded myself that I was a strong, smart woman.

You're even stronger and smarter now, KishaLynn.

Since I was now grown, it was time to act grown and move on. I told myself just to be grateful that I didn't get pregnant, or catch something permanent like herpes, HPV, or something deadly like HIV.

Fuck This Nigga. Fuck me for fucking This Nigga and for having the audacity to love him.

When I got back to campus after the holiday break, I was everywhere and nowhere on the inside. I went through the motions during the day, numb as if This Nigga had robbed me of the capacity to feel everything. But the pain found me every night. Betrayal and heartbreak lined up on my pillow and took turns getting punch-drunk off of tears I sobbed quietly, so I didn't disturb my two roommates. I isolated myself from Simone and my other few friends. I thought I deserved to suffer alone, as I had my entire life, with nothing to heal me and with no one to help me.

I was sure even Jesus had abandoned me with my sins. I thank God that I was wrong about that.

###

Epilogue: Save Me

Spring was blooming in Atlanta during the second semester of my freshman year in college, but my heart hadn't healed from its winter frostbite.

I started praying again, hoping to be heard through the sheath of sin that covered me.

I wrote a prayer mantra in my journal:

Dear God, if You hear me, please take this pain away. I'll do anything You say, Lord, just take this pain away. I know You can hear me pray Lord. Please take this pain away. Take this pain away Lord. I'll do anything You say.

One evening I was alone in my dorm room, praying this prayer when there came a knock on the door. I opened it to find a girl I had never seen before standing there. She was tall and skinny, with light brown, pimply skin, pulled back hair and modest clothes. She smiled at me as if she knew me.

"May I help you?" I asked, figuring she was lost or at the wrong door.

"Yes. I was just wondering what you're doing tonight?"

I was confused. “Do I know you?” I asked.

“No. Sorry, I’m Arlene.” She stuck her hand out to me. I shook it.

“KishaLynn. Nice to meet you.”

“Very nice indeed KishaLynn!” She replied with enthusiasm. “So, tonight...are you busy?”

Now I was curious. “Not exactly. Why?”

"My Church, New Birth, is having bible study tonight. Would you like to come with me? A shuttle bus will be here in a few minutes to take us there and back."

She smiled at me again. For the first time in a long time, I felt warmth fall over me, like a beam of sunshine breaking through a hole in the clouds.

I’ll do anything You say, Lord, just take this pain away.

“Yes, I’ll go," I said.

I pardoned myself to grab my purse and a jacket, and then I left my room, following Arlene down the hall and stairs. When we stepped outside, the winter sky was already dark and chilly. I silently followed her to the front gate of campus where a large group of students was boarding a fancy charter bus.

“What dorm do you stay in?” I asked Arlene as we got in the line to board.

"I don't go to Spelman. I go to Clark Atlanta."

"Oh! Well, what brought you to my dorm room door from the other side of the Atlanta University Center?" I asked.

"Jesus did," she said with a grin. "After you, KishaLynn."

I know You can hear me pray Lord. Please take this pain away.

Asking no more questions, I stepped past her onto the bus and rode it back to salvation.

###

THIS IS NOT THE END…

About The Author

KishaLynn Moore Elliott is a writer, speaker and certified life coach. She is the author of A D.R.E.A.M. Comes True, and CHILDISH, which is based on true stories from her childhood. She currently lives in San Diego with her wife and son. She graduated from Spelman College in 2002.

Made in the USA
Lexington, KY
22 November 2019

57503642R00146